CURRICULUM DEVELOPED BY JEREMY M

A COMPASSIONATE CALL TO

COUNTER CULTURE

IN A WORLD OF

POVERTY · SAME-SEX MARRIAGE · RACISM
SEX SLAVERY · IMMIGRATION · PERSECUTION
ABORTION · ORPHANS · PORNOGRAPHY

DAVID PLATT
NEW YORK TIMES BESTSELLING AUTHOR

LifeWay Press® Nashville, Tennessee

Published by LifeWay Press® • © 2015 David Platt

ISBN 978-1-4300-3860-3 • Item 005703478

Dewey decimal classification: 261
Subject headings: CHRISTIANITY AND CURRENT ISSUES \
CHURCH AND SOCIAL PROBLEMS \BIBLE. N.T. GOSPELS

Photo of David Platt: Allison Lewis

To order additional copies of this resource, write to LifeWay Church
Resources Customer Service; One LifeWay Plaza; Nashville, TN 37234-
0113; order online at www.lifeway.com; fax 615.251.5933; phone toll free
800.458.2772; email orderentry@lifeway.com; or visit the LifeWay Christian
Store serving you.

Printed in the United States of America

Adult Ministry Publishing • LifeWay Church Resources
One LifeWay Plaza • Nashville, TN 37234-0152

CONTENTS

THE AUTHOR

Dr. David Platt, the president of the International Mission Board, is deeply devoted to Christ and His Word. David's first love in ministry is making disciples and sharing, showing, and teaching God's Word in everyday life. He has traveled extensively to serve alongside church leaders throughout the United States and around the world.

A lifelong learner, David has earned two undergraduate and three advanced degrees. He holds a bachelor of arts and bachelor of arts in journalism from the University of Georgia and a master of divinity, a master of theology, and a doctor of philosophy from New Orleans Baptist Theological Seminary.

David previously served at New Orleans Baptist Theological Seminary as the dean of chapel and an assistant professor of expository preaching and apologetics, the staff evangelist at Edgewater Baptist Church in New Orleans, and the senior pastor of The Church at Brook Hills in Birmingham, Alabama. David has written several books, including *Radical, Radical Together, Follow Me,* and *Counter Culture.*

David founded Radical *(Radical.net),* a ministry devoted to serving churches and disseminating disciple-making resources to make the gospel known in all nations.

David and his wife, Heather, have four children: Caleb, Joshua, Mara Ruth, and Isaiah.

INTRODUCTION

On popular issues like poverty and slavery, about which Christians are likely to be applauded for our social action, we're quick to stand up and speak out. Yet on controversial issues like homosexuality and abortion, about which Christians are likely to be criticized for our social action, we're content to sit down and stay quiet.

It's as if we've decided to pick and choose which social issues we'll contest in our culture and which we'll concede. And our picking and choosing normally revolves around what's most comfortable—and least costly—for us.

What if the main issue isn't poverty or sex trafficking, homosexuality or abortion? What if the main issue is God? What if the main issue is the glory of God revealed in the gospel? And what might happen if we made Him our focus instead of a particular social issue?

In a world marked by sex slavery and sexual immorality, the abandonment and murder of children, racism and persecution, the needs of the poor and the neglect of the widow, how would we act if we fixed our gaze on the holiness, love, goodness, truth, justice, authority, and mercy of God as revealed in the gospel? How would our approach to social issues change?

So my aim in this Bible study is to call us to a contrite, compassionate but courageous response on the battle lines in our culture with the gospel. This Bible study is aimed toward helping one another think through how to apply the gospel consistently in our culture in such a way that we're able to speak the gospel clearly to our culture.

HOW TO GET THE MOST FROM THIS STUDY

ATTEND EACH GROUP EXPERIENCE.

WATCH the video teaching.

PARTICIPATE in the group discussions.

COMPLETE THE MATERIAL IN THIS BIBLE STUDY BOOK.

READ the daily lessons and **COMPLETE** the learning activities.

MEMORIZE each week's suggested memory verse.

BE HONEST with yourself and others about your thoughts, your questions, and your experiences as you study and apply the material.

ASK GOD to show you His truth about each topic so that you can boldly yet humbly counter culture with the gospel.

OBTAIN AND READ THE BOOK *COUNTER CULTURE* BY DAVID PLATT.

Tyndale, 2015, ISBN 978-1-4143-7329-4

TIPS FOR LEADING A SMALL GROUP

PRAYERFULLY PREPARE.

Prepare for each meeting by—

REVIEWING the weekly material and group questions ahead of time;

PRAYING for each person in the group.

Ask the Holy Spirit to work through you and the group discussion as you point to Jesus each week through God's Word.

MINIMIZE DISTRACTIONS.

Create a comfortable environment. If group members are uncomfortable, they'll be distracted and therefore not engaged in the group experience. Plan ahead by taking into consideration—

SEATING;

TEMPERATURE;

LIGHTING;

FOOD OR DRINK;

SURROUNDING NOISE;

GENERAL CLEANLINESS (put away pets if meeting in a home).

At best, thoughtfulness and hospitality show guests and group members they're welcome and valued in whatever environment you choose to gather. At worst, people may never notice your effort, but they're also not distracted. Do everything in your ability to help people focus on what's most important: connecting with God, with the Bible, and with others.

INCLUDE OTHERS.

Your goal is to foster a community in which people are welcome just as they are but encouraged to grow spiritually. Always be aware of opportunities to—

INVITE new people to join your group;

INCLUDE any people who visit the group.

An inexpensive way to make first-time guests feel welcome or to invite someone to get involved is to give them their own copies of this Bible study book.

ENCOURAGE DISCUSSION.

A good small group experience has the following characteristics.

EVERYONE PARTICIPATES. Encourage everyone to ask questions, share responses, or read aloud.

NO ONE DOMINATES—NOT EVEN THE LEADER. Be sure your time speaking as a leader takes up less than half of your time together as a group. Politely guide discussion if anyone dominates.

NOBODY IS RUSHED THROUGH QUESTIONS. Don't feel that a moment of silence is a bad thing. People often need time to think about their responses to questions they've just heard or to gain courage to share what God is stirring in their hearts.

INPUT IS AFFIRMED AND FOLLOWED UP. Make sure you point out something true or helpful in a response. Don't just move on. Build community with follow-up questions, asking how other people have experienced similar things or how a truth has shaped their understanding of God and the Scripture you're studying. People are less likely to speak up if they fear that you don't actually want to hear their answers or that you're looking for only a certain answer.

GOD AND HIS WORD ARE CENTRAL. Opinions and experiences can be helpful, but God has given us the truth. Trust Scripture to be the authority and God's Spirit to work in people's lives. You can't change anyone, but God can. Continually point people to the Word and to active steps of faith.

KEEP CONNECTING.

Think of ways to connect with group members during the week. Participation during the group session is always improved when members spend time connecting with one another outside the group sessions. The more people are comfortable with and involved in one another's lives, the more they'll look forward to being together. When people move beyond being friendly to truly being friends who form a community, they come to each session eager to engage instead of merely attending.

Encourage group members with thoughts, commitments, or questions from the session by connecting through—

EMAILS;

TEXTS;

SOCIAL MEDIA.

When possible, build deeper friendships by planning or spontaneously inviting group members to join you outside your regularly scheduled group time for—

MEALS;

FUN ACTIVITIES;

PROJECTS AROUND YOUR HOME, CHURCH, OR COMMUNITY.

CULTURE

WELCOME EVERYONE TO YOUR FIRST GROUP DISCUSSION OF *COUNTER CULTURE*.

Culture is defined as the beliefs, customs, arts, etc., of a particular society, group, place, or time.[1]

Where did you grow up? How would you describe the culture in which you grew up?

How would you describe the general culture of where we live today?

Describe a time when you felt that you clearly didn't fit in. (For example: You thought it was a costume party. You sat in the opposing team's section. You went to the wrong class. You couldn't speak the language. You didn't understand an international custom. You got lost.)

As followers of Christ, we won't always fit into the world in which we live. In fact, we'll find ourselves going against the flow of popular culture in certain areas of life. This Bible study will provide a solid biblical foundation to stand on in the midst of a rapidly shifting cultural landscape. The goal of this study is to understand how the eternal Word of God shapes our understanding of current issues and how we can share the gospel compassionately and courageously with the people around us.

To prepare to view the DVD segment, read aloud Romans 12:2.

Do not be conformed to this world, but be transformed by the renewal of your mind, that by testing you may discern what is the will of God, what is good and acceptable and perfect.
Romans 12:2

1. *www.merriam-webster.com/culture*

COMPLETE THE VIEWER GUIDE BELOW AS YOU WATCH DVD SESSION 1.

These days in our culture require authentic _____, real passion for God.

TWO PRAYERS FROM ACTS 17

1. God, make us zealous for Your _____.

  • _____ of the universe

  • _____ of life

  • _____ of the nations

  • _____ of the needy

  • _____ of each of us

  • _____ over all of us

  • _____ of the world

2. God, make us passionate for people's _____.

Let's _____ the gospel clearly.

FIVE TRUTHS OF THE GOSPEL

1. The _____ of God: God is the holy, just, and gracious Creator of all things.

2. The _____ of man: we're each created by God, but we're all corrupted by sin.

3. The _____ of Christ: Jesus alone is able to remove our sin and reconcile us to God.

4. The _____ of faith: the way to be reconciled to God is through faith in Jesus.

5. The _____ of eternity: our eternal destiny is dependent on our response to Jesus.

Let's _____ the gospel completely.

Video sessions available for purchase at *www.lifeway.com/counterculture*

DISCUSS THE DVD SEGMENT WITH YOUR GROUP, USING THE QUESTIONS BELOW.

What was most helpful, encouraging, or challenging in this session? Why?

On what social issues are you most likely to be courageous, outspoken, and active? Why?

On what social issues are you most likely to remain silent, uncertain, or inactive? Why?

Explain what David meant by "Our supposed social justice becomes a selective social injustice."

What relationship exists between action on social issues and a desire for God's glory? What do silence and inaction communicate?

In Acts 17:16-34 why is it significant to see Paul as a Christian explaining his beliefs rather than as a preacher?

When have you felt or been told that you were arrogant or had no right to tell other people what you believe to be true?

Explain what David shared about truth and love not being arrogant. How does this perspective give you courage and compassion?

Why are both courage and compassion important in addressing controversial social issues? Which comes easier to you—courage or compassion?

THIS WEEK

This week be prayerfully aware of points of commonality and points of conflict between the gospel and our culture. Memorize Romans 12:2 and practice summarizing the five truths of the gospel in a conversational presentation that could be shared in about one minute.

READ week 1 and complete the activities before the next group experience.
READ the introduction and chapter 1 in the book *Counter Culture* by David Platt (Tyndale, 2015).

CULTURE

Do not be conformed to this world, but be transformed by the renewal of your mind, that by testing you may discern what is the will of God, what is good and acceptable and perfect.
Romans 12:2

"If I profess, with the loudest voice and the clearest exposition, every portion of the truth of God except precisely that little point which the world and the devil are at that moment attacking, I am not confessing Christ, however boldly I may be professing Christianity. Where the battle rages the loyalty of the soldier is proved; and to be steady on all the battle-field besides is mere flight and disgrace to him if he flinches at that point."[1]
Elizabeth Rundle Charles

"A zealous man in religion is pre-eminently a man of one thing. It is not enough to say that this person is earnest, hearty, uncompromising, thorough-going, whole-hearted, fervent in spirit. He only sees one thing, he cares for one thing, he lives for one thing, he is swallowed up in one thing; and that one thing is to please God. Whether he lives, or whether he dies—whether he has health, or whether he has sickness—whether he is rich, or whether he is poor—whether he pleases man, or whether he gives offence—whether he is thought wise, or whether he is thought foolish—whether he gets blame, or whether he gets praise—whether he gets honour, or whether he gets shame—for all this the zealous man cares nothing at all. He burns for one thing; and that one thing is to please God, and to advance God's glory. If he is consumed in the very burning, he cares not for it—he is content. He feels that, like a lamp, he is made to burn; and if consumed in burning, he has but done the work for which God appointed him."[2]
J. C. Ryle

This week we'll lay foundations of the gospel and culture. Ultimately, we'll find answers to this important question: Why must Christians engage culture and, specifically, controversial issues?

1. Elizabeth Rundle Charles, *Chronicles of the Schönberg-Cotta Family,* vol. 1 (London: T. Nelson and Sons, 1864), 276.

2. John Charles Ryle, *Practical Religion* (Library of Alexandria, 2002), 130–31.

IN THE BEGINNING

The initial affront of the gospel is that there's a God by, through, and for whom all things begin. Because all things begin with God and ultimately exist for God, nothing in all creation or in our lives is irrelevant to Him. What we believe and what we do (or don't do) matter.

Read Genesis 1:1 and John 1:1-4.

What do the opening words of the Book of Genesis and the Gospel of John reveal about God?

That God was there in the beginning and that he created everything for himself. Nothing that is made was made apart from God.

In what ways is the existence of God increasingly controversial? In what ways is the reality of God as Creator even more controversial in today's culture?

How does rejecting the existence of God or simply rejecting Him as Creator radically alter a person's perspective on life, morality, and culture?

✸ **What other than God as Creator does your culture look to as a standard for authority, morality, and truth? At what point does that standard break down in its logic?**

The European union voted that life does not exist before birth.

Keep reading the opening pages of human history, and you'll see the ultimate problem of the human heart. The story began with God in His goodness creating mankind and giving great freedom. But that freedom was quickly abused:

> *The LORD God took the man and put him in the garden of Eden to work it and keep it. And the LORD God commanded the man, saying, "You may surely eat of every tree of the garden, but of the tree of the knowledge of good and evil you shall not eat, for in the day that you eat of it you shall surely die."*
> Genesis 2:15-17

In these verses God's holiness, goodness, justice, and grace are on display. God had the authority to define what's right and wrong, good and evil, based on His pure and holy character. God made clear to man that he'd be judged based on his obedience (or disobedience) to the command God had given. God's grace is evident in the fact that He didn't hide His law from His creation. In love God told man the way to life and exhorted him to walk in it.

Read Genesis 2:25.

What does this simple description reveal about life according to God's design?

That without knowledge of evil, even nakedness was innocent and shameless. God wanted everything to be perfect and was designed perfect until sin entered the world.

Read Genesis 3:1-7.

Describe what happened before the first man and woman disobeyed God.

They knew the commands of the Lord and obeyed them but felt like ~~they~~ they were being left out.

How does this scene establish a pattern at the root of all brokenness in the world?

They questioned God. They thought that they knew better than he did.

Describe the change between Genesis 2:25 and Genesis 3:7.

Write a definition of *sin* and an explanation of its consequences, based on this scene.

Sin is the willful disobedience of God because we elevate ourselves to a level equal to God and try to have equal authority. The consequence is death and eternal seperation from God.

Do you see the role reversal here? It all began when a command from God was reduced to questions about God: Is God really holy? Does He really know what's right? Is God really good? Does He really want what's best for me? Amid such questions man and woman subtly asserted themselves not as the ones to be judged by God but as the ones who sat in judgment of God.

The serpent's question revolved around the tree of the knowledge of good and evil. We may read the tree's name and think, *What's so wrong with knowing the difference between good and evil?* But the meaning of Scripture here goes beyond simple information about good and evil to the determination of good and evil. In other words, for man and woman to eat from this tree was to reject God as the One who determines good and evil and to assume this responsibility themselves. The temptation in the garden was to rebel against God's authority and in the process to make man the arbiter of morality.

When we understand the anatomy of this first sin, we realize that the moral relativism of the 21st century is nothing new. Once we take God out of the picture, we lose objectivity for determining what's good and evil, right and wrong, moral and immoral. Any argument for morality or goodness apart from our Creator eventually breaks down. Who's to say what's good or evil, right or wrong, for another individual or culture without the standard of God's design? So let's take a closer look at authority, an ongoing point of conflict in our culture.

(margin note, handwritten, left side) we choose God of Evil besides God

SHARING WHAT WE (DON'T) BELIEVE

Our culture is increasingly secular and humanistic, denying the very existence of God. One way to counter culture, as surprising as it may seem at first, is to build on common ground and points of agreement. Paul did this in Acts 17:23 when he used the cultural belief in an unknown god to share what he knew about a relationship with the one true God.

People who don't believe in God generally have a distorted perspective or misunderstanding of who God is. For example, they might say they don't believe in an angry old man in the sky waiting to smite everyone who does something wrong. You can agree that this idea isn't true about God as revealed in the Bible. Allowing them to express what they don't believe will often reveal a point of agreement between you. After they've shared what they believe or don't believe about God, they're often more likely to return the favor, allowing you to share what you believe about Him.

You may be surprised to find that people are open to hear what you believe if you start by allowing them to share what they don't believe and by affirming the views you share in common. Many people expect Christians to be combative and defensive. To be fair, many of us have earned that reputation. My prayer is that this study will help you engage people in a way that creates openness to the truth of God.

Identify common objections to belief in God or Christianity.

Old man in the sky
Someone who. Controls your mind.
Hypocrites

Write a simple response to those objections, starting with ways you agree that something isn't true and moving to what you believe to be true about God.

DAY 2
IDOLATRY

"I could not endure existence if Jesus was not glorified; it would be hell to me, if he were to be always ... dishonored."[1] —Henry Martyn

As a missionary in India, Henry Martyn was literally surrounded by idolatry in a culture filled with thousands of gods. And while our culture may not be as blatant in its worship of man-made gods as the one Henry was immersed in to share the gospel, our culture is no less idolatrous. In some ways idolatry can be even more dangerous and deceptive in our culture because we often don't realize we're worshiping other things. We bow before them, so to speak, when we look to them for our hope, meaning, satisfaction, comfort, pleasure, or prosperity and when we think they'll make our lives better. This is nothing less than idolatry.

From the beginning of human history until now, our natural human tendency has been to glorify things other than God. This pattern of sin has been repeated throughout every generation and every day since the garden of Eden.

Just as Henry Martyn had an overwhelming desire to see Jesus honored, Paul wasn't content to believe in God while the culture around Him glorified other things. Let's look back at part of the story from our group session that describes Paul's visit to the city of Athens.

Read Acts 17:16-21.

Besides the blatant idolatry evident in this passage, we see a more subtle idolatry in the Athenians' mindset. In verse 21 below, circle the words *all, spend their time, nothing except,* and *something new.*

Now all the Athenians and the foreigners who lived there would spend their time in nothing except telling or hearing something new.
Acts 17:21

What examples of this form of idolatry—obsessing over new things—do you see in our culture?

New technology
New TV shows
New cars
New Houses

You are surrounded by a culture similar to the one of Athens. You also have a marketplace—places you go and people with whom you interact in your daily routines. This marketplace is your mission field. These are God-given opportunities to share your life and share the gospel.

What's your marketplace? Identify routines and people in your circles of influence.

Places I regularly go:

Super market
work
school

People with whom I regularly interact:

Paul was stirred to holy anger by the idolatry surrounding him (see v. 16). Identifying what makes you angry can help you pinpoint what you're truly passionate about. It can reveal to you a source of zeal—even an object of worship. The reason you get angry is that what matters most to you is being threatened or neglected in some way. If it's anything other than God, you're identifying a god or an idol in your heart.

The heart of every Christian should burn with desire for God's glory. We can't sit back and remain silent while God isn't glorified and people are on a path that ultimately leads to self-destruction. A life given over to misguided desires; selfish ambition; and a relentless pursuit of new experiences, ideas, or possessions is simply unacceptable. We want more. Because people need it. And because God deserves it. He alone is worthy of our worship.

That's what Jesus taught His followers to pray, right?

Our Father in heaven,
hallowed be your name.
Matthew 6:9

We ask God to cause His name to be known as holy in my life, in my family, in the church, and in the culture around us. That desire should drive not only our personal prayers but also our public lives on a daily basis.

What makes you angry?

What does your answer reveal about your passion and your object of worship?

Biblically, putting anything other than God in a position of ultimate authority and highest affection is idolatry. Idols are more than physical objects of worship.

This is true not only of our culture or of people throughout the world but also of our individual lives. We worship all sorts of things, making them ultimate in authority and affection.

Read Romans 1:21-25.

Summarize the three great exchanges described in these verses. Then identify examples of the same exchanges that take place in our culture today.

	EXCHANGES	EXAMPLES TODAY
Thought:	Glory of God - mortal man.	
Worship:		
Desire:		

What's idolized in our culture? Make this list as extensive and specific as possible.

Sex   Cars
Food   Technology
money   Freedom.
Sports   Love
School

What are you tempted to idolize? Make this list as extensive and specific as possible.

Answer as you please

How would you explain worship to someone who doesn't consider himself religious or spiritual? Provide examples of secular worship and ways it's misdirected.

Talking about Sports
Searching out sports Statistics
watching hours of television.

Ironically, another subtle form of idolatry is to deny God's existence altogether. It happens when we worship ourselves, our own limited intellect, or an ideal and so-called greater good. We live in a culture that increasingly distances itself from religious labels and from religion in general. People are more and more likely to identify themselves as "other" or even as "none" when responding to questions about religious belief. Some wouldn't even bother to describe themselves as atheist or agnostic.

But to say there's no God is really an unsustainable negation. There's no way to prove God doesn't exist. Think about it. If you say something isn't there—for example, to say a certain object isn't in the room where you're reading this right now—then that means you've searched everywhere in the entire room to find whether it's possible that the thing is there. If you search the whole room and learn that it's not there, you can definitively say, "OK, it's not here."

It's impossible to apply this same argument to the existence of God. To say there's no God, you'd have to search all existence to see whether He's there. To do this, you'd have to be omnipresent, omnipotent, and omniscient; in other words, you yourself would have to be God. There's no way to definitively conclude that something doesn't exist that's beyond our human limitations. Therefore, to deny a transcendent Creator just isn't possible. Any reasonable person would have to admit that it's at least possible God exists.

Read Romans 1:18-20.

What did Paul write about people's knowledge of and accountability to God?

What emotions do you experience when you read the sobering reality of Romans 1:18-25? Why?

All people must decide whether they'll acknowledge and believe in God. The Bible is clear about this. You probably have opportunities to share the good news of Jesus during your daily routine. Pray that God will give you passion for His glory as you go throughout your day.

1. Henry Martyn, as quoted in Constance E. Padwick, *Henry Martyn: Confessor of the Faith* (IVF, 1953), 146.

DAY 3
ENGAGING CULTURE

For the sake of simplicity, let's say we can have one of four possible responses in engaging our culture.

1. **WE CONFORM.** We start compromising what we believe and the way we act in order to appeal to and appease the surrounding culture. We may even genuinely believe that doing so is both loving and strategic, hoping somehow people will be attracted to Jesus through a less offensive form of Christianity and will ultimately be saved. However, we have to realize that our goal isn't to make following Jesus easier. We'll look more closely tomorrow at the message of the gospel, but we've already seen that at its core, it's necessarily countercultural and offensive to the human heart.

2. WE CHECK OUT. The opposite extreme is to secede from culture, distancing ourselves so completely that we never have any interaction with the world around us. Again, the intent may seem honorable and sincere because we want to remove even an appearance of evil and the temptation of sin. But Jesus specifically prayed that His Father wouldn't take His followers out of the world but protect them while they were sent into it (see John 17:15-16). The world around us desperately needs the life-changing power of the gospel. Forming an isolated, insulated subculture may feel countercultural, but it isn't an appropriate response. Countering culture doesn't mean withdrawing and isolating ourselves from culture.

3. WE COMBAT. This approach is antagonistic and defensive. While the intent begins moving in the right direction, refusing to give in to or give up on the world around us, it misses the heart of Jesus. This response sees culture as an enemy to be defeated instead of people to be saved. Our desire mustn't be to prove ourselves right or to force our way on the world around us. Instead, our goal is to show Christ to be true and worthy. Just as wrong as running away from our culture is driving people away from the church. Countering culture doesn't mean attacking it.

4. WE COUNTER. Countering culture means engaging culture with conviction and compassion. We stand firmly on the truth of God, empowered by the Spirit, to extend the love of Christ to a lost and dying world. Our desire isn't to conquer but to redeem. It matters what we do, how we do it, and why we do it.

A wrong response to culture is more than unhealthy or unhelpful. It's potentially damning. Engaging our culture is literally a matter of life or death—eternal life or death.

This dynamic is precisely what we see in Paul's interaction with the people of Athens in the synagogue, the marketplace, and the Areopagus. Yesterday we focused on what exactly provoked a response from Paul. Tomorrow we'll focus on the content of his response. Today let's look at the spirit of his response—how he engaged culture.

Read Acts 17:22-34.

What were the various responses to what Paul shared?

He was mocked, some sought to know more, others believed.

As noted in the video, we can hardly consider the response to be a great revival. However, Paul was effective in engaging people, and consequently, at least some believed—both men and women.

? What's your greatest fear about engaging people with the countercultural message of Jesus?

Fear of rejection
Fear that perhaps it isnt true?

What would you consider success in sharing your beliefs?

Having people submit their lives to Christ.

Notice that Paul showed respect and identified points of agreement but also spoke clearly about points of disagreement and wasn't shy to call out error. His speech is an invaluable example of how to counter culture with conviction and compassion.

What specific examples do you see of Paul's showing respect and building agreement?

He talked about how religious they were and about the Statute to the unknown God .

What specific examples do you see of Paul's challenging people's beliefs?

He pointed out that we are Gods offspring and thus we cant be from a God made of gold or Silver .

Paul was familiar enough with the culture in Athens to quote a pagan poet. He identified points of common interest and shared values or ideals as ways to introduce the truth of the gospel.

How can you use popular expressions of art, such as music, movies, books, and shows, to understand culture and to share the gospel?

Take me to Church Song
walking Dead

Try it now. Identify a popular song, show, or movie.

Based on what you identified, what desires, needs, questions, or values do you see or hear expressed in popular culture?

How can those desires, needs, questions, or values be fulfilled or answered in Jesus?

Also note what Paul didn't do. He didn't boycott idol makers or petition for legislation to be passed against them. He didn't scold or shame them.

Identify examples of Christians combating culture in ways that sought to force a position without heart change.

What was the result of the combative activity?

What could have been done differently?

To be clear, we should absolutely utilize the freedoms we have in social and political systems. However, believers don't rely on a political party, a government program, or another form of activism to change our world. We put our hope entirely in our Savior and Redeemer. Jesus' kingdom isn't of this world (see John 18:36). The rights we exercise and the actions we take should be done in a spirit of conviction and compassion. We act in humility and love. Not judgment. Not with a mean spirit. Not to force anyone to conform to our values or beliefs. In love.

IT IS GOOD

You have a choice to make. Will you go with the flow of popular opinion and cultural trends? Or will you cling to the holy standard of God's Word? Will you seek what's most comfortable and take the path of least resistance? Or will you trust the loving authority of your Creator and His good design for all creation?

If you're truly going to be passionate about the glory of God, you have to believe in the depths of your heart that God's design is good. It's not enough to begrudgingly forfeit what you truly want from a sense of duty to submit to God's will. That's just a step away from where Adam and Eve were back in the garden. They listened to the lie of our Enemy, the whisper that caused them to question God's goodness. Do you believe God is holding back something good from you? Do you believe a sinful desire is truly good and satisfying in a way God isn't? Until you trust that God is good and His design is good, you'll be on the brink of giving in to outside pressure or inner desire, exchanging the truth for a lie, the Creator for creation. Don't settle for less than the good, pleasing, and perfect will of God.

Record the following verses.

John 10:10

Romans 12:2

James 1:16-17

How will these verses encourage and equip you to counter culture?

DAY 4
THE GOSPEL

The gospel doesn't simply compel us to confront culture; it causes conflict with culture. It stands in direct opposition to culture.

Consider the message of the gospel: the good news that the God of the universe has looked on relentlessly rebellious and hopelessly sinful men and women and has sent Jesus, God in the flesh, to bear His wrath against sin on the cross and to show His power over sin in the resurrection so that all who turn from themselves and trust in Him can be reconciled to God for all eternity. When you truly grasp the gravity of this message, you begin to realize that the gospel doesn't just compel Christians to confront social issues in the culture around us. The gospel itself creates confrontation with the culture around and within us.

Does the gospel create controversy?

Now we see the offense of the gospel coming to the forefront. Tell any modern person that there's a God who sustains, owns, defines, rules, and will one day judge him or her, and that person will balk in offense. Any man or woman would—and every man and woman has. This is our natural reaction to God.

The past couple of days you've read about Paul's response to idolatry and the way he engaged culture. Today let's back up a couple of verses to see exactly what he said about the gospel in the context of a culture filled with idolatry and sensuality.

Read Romans 1:16-17.

In what ways are you ashamed of the gospel?

Summarize Paul's rationale for not being ashamed of the gospel.

It is the power of Salvation for All who believe.

The very fact that Paul felt it necessary to write about not being ashamed of the gospel suggests either that he faced pressure to feel ashamed and keep quiet or that the gospel was considered shameful by some. Paul had been a Pharisee, so his former peers and other Jewish adherents would have considered his radical change in life and message shameful.

What encouragement does Paul's statement provide for you today?

It's vital to understand what the gospel is—both for your sake and for the sake of others around you. Unfortunately, the word *gospel* has become a religious buzzword lately, meaning it tends to gets thrown around a lot or added to all kinds of concepts and phrases. To be clear, our lives and churches should absolutely be centered on the gospel. We should preach, teach, and live out the gospel in our homes, in our communities, in our workplaces, and around the world. But adding the word *gospel* to something, doesn't mean what we're actually doing has anything to do with the message of Jesus, nor does it mean people understand what the gospel is or how something relates to the gospel. So for the rest of our study today, let's walk through the five truths we saw in Acts 17 that make up the whole gospel message. The goal is not only to reiterate them biblically but also to grow comfortable explaining each truth in your own words so that you'll be ready when opportunities arise to share the gospel naturally with family members, friends, coworkers, neighbors, and other acquaintances.

FIVE GOSPEL TRUTHS

1. The character of God. God is the holy, just, and gracious Creator of all things.

Read Acts 17:24-31.

What attributes did Paul mention to describe God's character?

Creator, He does not live in temples, nor is he served by Human hands, He gives to everyone, He is close to us, He is Righteous, He is a Judge.

What other attributes would you use to describe God's character? Include Scripture references.

2. The sinfulness of man. We're each created by God, but we're all corrupted by sin.

Read Romans 1:18-25; 3:23.

How would you explain man's sinfulness?

Everyone knows God but rejects him. They do not honor God, Men claim to be wise yet are fools, They worshiped Idols instead of God and were perveted to do impure things because the exchanged the truth of God for a lie.

What examples would you provide of your own sinfulness?

I was a drus addict, porn addict, hater,

3. The sufficiency of Christ. Jesus alone is able to remove our sin and reconcile us to God.

Read Romans 3:24-25; 5:19-21; 6:23.

How would you explain the sufficiency of Christ?

Christ, being sinless, was a sufficeint sacrifice to take all the sins of the world upon himself.

Before you knew Christ, how did you try to improve your life or make yourself good enough for the approval of God or others? Where did you put your hope?

4. The necessity of faith. We're reconciled to God only through faith in Jesus.

Read Romans 5:1-2; Ephesians 2:1-10; and Hebrews 11:6.

How would you explain the necessity of faith?

Only through Faith in Jesus are we able to be reconciled to God the Father.

Describe the moment when you realized your need to trust Jesus for salvation.

5. The urgency of eternity. Our eternal destiny depends on our response to Jesus.

Read Matthew 7:21-23; 25:46; and John 3:16.
How would you explain the relationship between the urgency of eternity and the need to respond to the gospel?

How does a view of eternity shape your daily priorities?

How does it provide courage to share the gospel?

THE GOSPEL ISN'T A RELIGIOUS SALES PITCH.

IT'S A DEEPLY PERSONAL STORY OF LOVE AND SALVATION.

DAY 5
SPEAKING UP

If you really believe the gospel, you'll share the gospel. You have to speak up.

We can't sit idly by while literally billions of people in the world are heading toward eternal judgment. Like Paul (see Acts 17:16), we should be provoked. We should be stirred to action, knowing that people all around us aren't giving God the glory He deserves and aren't receiving the grace He offers. These aren't faceless numbers—impersonal statistics. Right now, as you read this, people you know, human beings created in the image of God, are headed for an eternal crisis. Considering that people you know and love need to be saved, can you afford to remain silent?

Read Romans 10:9-13.

Who can be saved?

All who call upon the name of the Lord!

What's required for salvation? *Repentence.*
Belief
Confession
This is not Just a simple acknouledgement

Is there anyone in your life about whom you've honestly felt, "They'll never believe. They're too far gone to be saved"? Record the names of people in your life who don't currently believe in Jesus as their Savior and Lord. Pause now to pray for God to work miraculously in their lives and to use you to share the good news of salvation.

Devin
Shawn

but a heartfelt personal conviction, wrthot reservation that Jesus is the master and is soverign over thier life.

Read Romans 10:14-15.

What emotions do you experience as you read Paul's series of rhetorical questions?

What's your role in salvation?

To bear the good news of Jesus

Read Romans 10:16-17.

Notice that *obey* and *believe* are used interchangeably in these verses. Explain the relationship between action and belief in being saved by faith.

To truly believe in God one must obey.

Using the logic presented in these verses, what responsibility do you have to speak the gospel? Why isn't it enough to merely be nice, moral citizens and neighbors in hopes that people will be attracted to Jesus without your having to speak the gospel?

ONE WAY

Paul was clear that salvation comes only through faith in Christ as presented in the gospel. This means that Christians believe in absolute truth and that all religions and philosophies aren't equally good and acceptable. I probably don't have to tell you that talking about Jesus as the only way to be saved is considered narrow-minded and even hateful in our culture.

Jesus spoke one of the most radical statements in all human history on the night before His crucifixion. The words He lovingly shared with His disciples are just as true and as countercultural today as they were two thousand years ago:

> *Jesus said to him, "I am the way, and the truth, and the life. No one comes to the Father except through me."*
> John 14:6

Why does our culture find it hateful and narrow-minded to believe that Jesus is the only true God and the one way to experience eternal life? What idol does this reveal?

When have you felt or been told that you were arrogant or self-righteous for sharing your faith in Jesus as the only way to a right relationship with God?

Devin

Why would the epitome of hate be refusing to share the gospel?

you are dooming people to hell!

To believe we're somehow superior to someone else or more deserving of God's love than another culture or people group would be arrogant. But that's not what we believe. To believe billions of people need to believe what we believe or they'll spend eternity in hell would be hateful—unless it's true. If the gospel is true—and it is—then we must share it with everyone. It isn't hateful or narrow-minded to warn someone of impending danger or death. It's hateful and selfish *not* to warn and plead with others, seeking to convince them of the only way to have life.

If a building caught on fire and you knew the only way out, the most loving and selfless thing you could do would be to tell others how they can be saved. On an eternal scale this is exactly what's happening. No matter how hard they work, how noble their efforts, or how far they actually get through that burning building, if only one way to salvation exists, everything they've done and everyone who's followed them will perish. You can't simply be nice and hope people ask whether you know the way out. You have to tell people there's only one way, one truth, and one life. Otherwise, nobody will be saved. In this scenario it's easy to see that worrying about whether the message will be appreciated or socially acceptable is crazy.

It's a lie from the Enemy to believe you should be quiet and let other people believe whatever works for them. Ultimately, anything other than faith in the gospel won't work for anyone.

APPLYING THE GOSPEL

The hope and prayer is that this study will equip you to tie pressing social issues to the gospel and will empower you to use these issues to speak about the gospel to those who need to hear it. As a result, you won't sit back in paralyzed silence the next time someone in your workplace brings up a controversial issue, but instead, you'll seize this opportunity to bring the gospel to bear on that issue and address the most significant need in every person's heart.

Helping the poor gives us an opportunity to communicate how Christ, though He was rich, became poor so that others could become rich (see 2 Cor. 8:9). Caring for orphans provides us an opportunity to tell people that God pursues us as His children and adopts us into His family through Christ (see Rom. 8:15-17; Gal. 4:1-7). Defending marriage in our culture provides us an opportunity to show that God designed the relationship of a husband and a wife to illustrate Christ's love for His people on the cross (see Eph. 5:22-33). Working against racism in our culture provides us an opportunity to share how Christ came to redeem people from every tribe, tongue, and nation to belong to Him (see Rev. 5:9-10; 7:9-10). All these issues open the door for the gospel to come in and change lives forever.

As we begin to look at specific social issues, it's vital that you get ready to clearly articulate the gospel. Before you can apply the gospel in life and conversation, make sure you know what it is.

Record a simple presentation of the gospel that includes the five gospel truths you studied yesterday: the character of God, the sinfulness of man, the sufficiency of Christ, the necessity of faith, and the urgency of eternity.

IF YOU REALLY BELIEVE THE GOSPEL,

YOU'LL SPEAK UP AND SHARE IT.

WEALTH

WELCOME EVERYONE TO THIS SECOND GROUP DISCUSSION OF *COUNTER CULTURE*.

What was most helpful, encouraging, or challenging in your study of week 1?

 What issues of wealth or poverty have you seen in the news or on social media lately? Share a recent news story related to wealth, poverty, orphans, or widows.

To prepare to view the DVD segment, read aloud Mark 12:28-31.

One of the scribes came up and heard them disputing with one another, and seeing that he answered them well, asked him, "Which commandment is the most important of all?" Jesus answered, "The most important is, 'Hear, O Israel: The Lord our God, the Lord is one. And you shall love the Lord your God with all your heart and with all your soul and with all your mind and with all your strength.' The second is this: 'You shall love your neighbor as yourself.' There is no other commandment greater than these."
Mark 12:28-31

COMPLETE THE VIEWER GUIDE BELOW AS YOU WATCH DVD SESSION 2.

Over _____ _____ people live and die in desperate poverty in the world, living on less than one dollar a day.

MATERIAL RICHES IN THE CHURCH

1. The path to great _____

   • Be content with having _____.

   • Be cautious with acquiring _____.

      You will take _____ of it with you.

      Excess will take _____ from you.

      You will miss God's _____ for you.

2. The path to total _____

   • Love of _____

   • Desire for _____

      The love of money and the desire for riches lead to a life of self-_____ and self-_____.

3. The plan for _____ people

   • Flee self-_____.

   • Flee self-_____.

   • Focus on _____.

      God gives good things for _____ enjoyment.

      We give good things for _____ enjoyment.

      We invest good things in our and others' _____.

WHAT THE GOSPEL COMPELS

1. Simplify your _____.

2. Increase your _____.

   • What is God leading you to _____?

   • What is God leading you to _____?

   • What is God leading you to _____?

3. Consider your _____.

Video sessions available for purchase at *www.lifeway.com/counterculture*

DISCUSS THE DVD SEGMENT WITH YOUR GROUP, USING THE QUESTIONS BELOW.

What was most helpful, encouraging, or challenging in this session? Why?

What emotions did you feel when hearing statistics and quotations related to poverty?

How does our culture view gain?

What countercultural perspective on wealth is presented in 1 Timothy 6?

How have you experienced the unquenchable thirst for more—comparable to drinking seawater? When did you get what you wanted, only to discover it didn't satisfy you or even made you worse off than before you got it?

Explain what David meant when he said that how we handle money can literally make or break us forever.

What insecurities arise when you consider not having your things? What does this reaction reveal?

Give examples of how godly contentment is great gain.

How does the gospel compel action related to wealth and poverty?

How do issues of poverty open a door to conversations about the gospel? Give examples of statements that relate the gospel to poverty, wealth, orphans, or widows.

THIS WEEK

Identify something you can share, sell, and sacrifice in order to love your neighbor as yourself. Memorize Luke 10:27 and continue praying for an awareness of the needs around you and discernment on how to respond.

READ week 2 and complete the activities before the next group experience.
READ chapters 2 and 4 in the book *Counter Culture* by David Platt (Tyndale, 2015).

WEALTH

> *He answered, "You shall love the Lord your God with all your heart and with all your soul and with all your strength and with all your mind, and your neighbor as yourself."*
> Luke 10:27

"*The Bible's teachings should cut to the heart of North American Christians. By any measure, we are the richest people ever to walk on planet Earth. Furthermore, at no time in history has there ever been greater economic disparity in the world than at present. … While the average American lives on more than ninety dollars per day, approximately one billion people live on less that one dollar per day and 2.6 billion—40 percent of the world's population—live on less than two dollars per day. … What is the task of the church? We are to embody Jesus Christ by doing what He did and what He continues to do through us: declare—using both words and deeds—that Jesus is the King of kings and Lord of lords who is bringing in a kingdom of righteousness, justice, and peace. And the church needs to do this where Jesus did it, among the blind, the lame, the sick and outcast, and the poor.*"[1]
Steve Corbett & Brian Fikkert

In this second week we'll begin to look more closely at how the gospel informs and influences our lives, particularly regarding our material blessings. What does it mean to love our neighbors as ourselves? How do we reflect God's heart in a world of poverty, orphans, and widows?

1. Steve Corbett & Brian Fikkert, *When Helping Hurts: How to Alleviate Poverty Without Hurting the Poor ... and Yourself* (Chicago, IL: Moody Publishers, 2012), 41.

DAY 1
ORPHANS, WIDOWS, THE POOR, & GOD

A concern for the poor isn't a recent fad or cultural trend. Although it's certainly wonderful that across our culture there are an increasing awareness of the needs of the poor and a desire to help them, we mustn't lose sight of the gospel as the foundation for our concern.

When you read the Bible, you see over and over God's passion to demonstrate His power and love in the lives of those in need.

Read Deuteronomy 10:17-18.

List every name or description of God and His character mentioned in these verses.

God of Gods
Lord of Lords
Great
mighty

Awesome
not partial
judge
giver

Read Psalm 68:5.

What two ways is God described?

Father to the Fatherless
Protector of the widow

Read Exodus 22:22.

In the initial giving of His law, what command did God give His people?

Not to mistreat the widow
or orphan

Read Isaiah 1:17.

List the specific instruction God gave His people through the prophet Isaiah.

Learn to do good which is the following:
- Seek justice
- correct oppression
- provide justice to the Fatherless
- plead the widows case

When we read these verses, we quickly notice that God's heart isn't just for the orphan but also for the widow. In each of these verses (and in many others), God groups these two classes of people together. It's no surprise, then, to come to this breathtaking verse later in the Bible.

Read James 1:27.

What's God's definition of *pure religion* (some translations may use *true religion*)? Record James 1:27 in the space below.

To visit the orphen. and. widows in their affliction & Keep oneself undefiled from the world

What an astounding statement. True religion doesn't consist of monotonous participation in superficial pious activity. True religion consists of just and consistent demonstrations of supernatural, selfless love.

When the Bible describes visiting orphans and widows here, it means more than simply saying hello to them every once in a while. This same word for *visit* in James 1:27 is used in different places in the New Testament to describe how God Himself visits His people to help them, strengthen them, and encourage them. To visit orphans and widows means to seek them out with a deep concern for their well-being and a clear commitment to care for their needs.

Why, we might wonder, *would God define pure religion in this particular way—in terms of care for orphans and widows?* The answer to that question is found in the second half of James 1:27, when James describes "[keeping] oneself unstained from the world." It's at this point that many people think, *OK, if I'm going to have true religion, then that means I need to care for orphans and widows, and then I need to avoid immorality in the world.* Of course it's true that we're to avoid immorality, and the rest of James elaborates on this theme in different ways. However, we need to be careful not to disconnect "[keeping] oneself unstained from the world" from "[visiting] orphans and widows." For in the verses right after James 1:27, James chides the church for catering to a world system that prioritizes the wealthy and neglects the needy. People who live according to the ways of the world, James says, give attention and honor to the kind of people who can benefit them the most, who have the most to offer them in return for their kindness. True religion, however, is unstained from this worldly way of thinking and living. True religion results in sacrificially caring for people who can benefit you the least, who have the least to offer you in return for your kindness.

Enter the orphan and the widow—children and women who've lost a significant member of their family on whom they depended for physical, emotional, relational, and spiritual sustenance. Consequently, they desperately need someone to step in and provide physical, emotional, relational, and spiritual sustenance to them. True religion, according to God, is to love people like that. True religion is to be family to those who've lost family.

So what does this mean for followers of Christ in a world of 153 million orphans?[1] Moreover, what shall we do in a world filled with 245 million widows, 115 million or more of whom live in poverty and suffer from social isolation and economic deprivation as a result of losing their husbands?[2] Knowing that each one of these millions represents a unique child or woman for whom God possesses divine compassion, it's not a question of what we should do. The only question is whether we'll do it.

How will you practice true religion? Use the following chart to identify possible opportunities and action steps.

VISIT ORPHANS	VISIT WIDOWS	KEEP UNSTAINED FROM THE WORLD

What's the Holy Spirit prompting you to do in response to this great need?

Even with increased awareness in our culture of the poor and orphaned, how is practicing true religion countercultural?

Describe the general attitude of our culture toward the poor and those who can't take care of themselves.

The implications of this teaching are mammoth for the church in contemporary culture. Now, possibly more than at any other point in history, the church has an opportunity to rise up and show God's love, not just to children and women whose parents or husbands have died but also to children and women whose parents or husbands have disappeared from their lives. Without question, the Father to the fatherless and the Defender of the widow is calling His people to care for these children and women like our own families.

Read Deuteronomy 15:4.

What did God expect from the community of His people in the Old Testament?

That they would use thier blessings of aboundance to ensure their has no poor cmong then

Read Acts 2:44-45; 4:34-35.

How is the first church described in the New Testament?

They lived as a family ready to take care of one another

Why is this a significant detail to include in the earliest descriptions of the church?

It paints a practical vision of whet we es the Church should look like -

The picture we have in the New Testament, from the very beginning of the church, is a community that's sacrificing for one another so that there's no needy person among them. Offerings were taken up for the church in Jerusalem in the middle of famine. Scripture, from cover to cover, talks about God's care for the poor, His concern for the outcast, and His intention for His people to reflect His compassion.

THROUGHOUT SCRIPTURE, FROM COVER TO COVER, GOD REVEALS HIS HEART AS A DEFENDER OF THE POOR AND A FATHER OF THE FATHERLESS.

1. "Christian Alliance for Orphans' White Paper on Understanding Orphan Statistics," Christian Alliance for Orphans [online, cited 26 November 2014]. Available from the Internet: *www.christianalliancefororphans.org.*
2. "Over 115 million widows worldwide live in poverty," *USA Today* [online], 23 June 2010 [cited 26 November 2014]. Available from the Internet: *usatoday.com.*

DAY 2
TREASURES

Our culture constantly reinforces a desire for more. We think, *I want more,* but we don't realize that the desire for riches is a trap, and the more we indulge this desire, the more it destroys our soul. And it may destroy us forever.

Read 1 Timothy 6:9-10.

In your own words, how would you summarize Paul's warning to Timothy?

To not seek after riches.

In what way do you struggle with a craving for and love of money?

I crave the ability to have enogh money to not have to worry about money

How have you seen the harmful and ruinous pangs of a desire for riches in our culture?

Goldman Sachs
AIG
WaMu

How have you seen the harmful and ruinous pangs of a desire for riches in your own life?

Credit Card
Debt

The comfort of riches is a subtle trap. It has a numbing effect on our lives that can eventually paralyze us spiritually. Not only are we often unwilling to move out of our comfort zones, taking steps of faith in God and compassion toward others, but we also may not even be aware of those needs and opportunities. We can even be lulled into a religious routine that blinds us to anything outside ourselves.

This tendency is something of which I became painfully aware in my own life. Let me give you a personal example. In the eyes of the world (even the church world), my family was living the dream. But deep down inside I had this sinking feeling that we were missing the point.

Conviction came to a head when our friends John and Abigail came to visit us in Birmingham. Years before, John and Abigail had sold everything they had and moved their family (with four young girls) to a North African country to declare and demonstrate God's love in the midst of massive poverty. They were back in the United States for a few months, and during that time they spent a couple of days with us. They shared stories of ways God was providing for their needs and the needs of the people they were working among. They spoke with great joy, even as they shared about the suffering they'd seen and the struggles they'd experienced.

As I listened to them in my large house, surrounded by all the comforts I'd acquired, I knew my friends possessed a faith with which I was unfamiliar. They never made a comment about the extravagance in which we were living, but I was cut to the core by a sacrificial compassion I saw in them that I didn't see in me. Sure, I was a pastor (and a successful one by all the standards the church culture around me had set) who read, studied, and preached God's Word. But when it came to the poor, I was word and talk, devoid of deed and truth. My lack of concern for the poor was a clear sign of a fundamental problem with my faith.

On a scale of 1 to 10 (1 = not concerned at all; 10 = completely heartbroken), how concerned for the poor would you say you are?

1	5	10

Where do your acts of compassion actually fall on this spectrum? Plot a second point above. Is it the same as what you say about your concern? Explain any difference.

When and where have you experienced the convicting work of the Spirit?

Thankfully, Scripture gives us a remedy when surrounded by riches. Right before the warnings in 1 Timothy, Scripture prescribes a simple life of contentment that prioritizes necessities and minimizes luxuries.

Read 1 Timothy 6:6-8.

Take a moment to identify the necessities and luxuries with which God has blessed you.

NECESSITIES	LUXURIES
Home Clothes Food Car	Cell phone TV Car Stuff Dogs

In the lists above, circle the things you can take with you "out of this world" (v. 7).

WARNINGS

The warnings are all over Scripture. Remember Achan in Joshua 7? He just wanted a few possessions from the plunder of war, so he hid them in his home. And as a result, he and his entire family died. It's not just the Old Testament. Jesus came on the scene and said it's hard for a rich man even to enter the kingdom of God (see Matt.19:23-24). In Luke 6 He said, "Woe to you who are rich, for you have received your consolation. Woe to you who are full now, for you shall be hungry" (vv. 24-25). James wrote these haunting words to the church:

> *Come now, you rich, weep and howl for the miseries are coming upon you. Your riches have rotted. Your garments are moth-eaten. Your gold and silver have corroded, and the corrosion will be evidence against you and will eat your flesh like fire. You have laid up treasure in the last days. You have lived on the earth in luxury and self-indulgence.*
> James 5:1-3,5

It's all over the Bible. Materialism is dangerous. And not just now but forever. It's dangerous, and it's damning.

INVEST ETERNALLY

Read 1 Timothy 6:17-19.

What does Paul say people should do with their possessions?

rich in good deeds
generous
willing to share.

Read Matthew 6:19-21.

Look back at the verses printed from James 5. Circle any similar language in James's and Jesus' warnings about riches.

Explain what's meant by *treasure*.

Its anything above your necessities

What are examples of earthly treasures in your life?

Car, Phone, Guns, Excess Food,

What does our culture encourage you to treasure?

Stuff or things

What does it mean to store up treasures in heaven?

Eternal deeds.

Clearly, Jesus has put before us a choice: we can spend our wealth on short-term pleasures that we can't keep, or we can sacrifice our wealth for long-term treasure that we'll never lose.

These words to the crowds remind me of my favorite part of Jesus' conversation with the rich young man. Jesus said to this wealthy ruler, "Go, sell all that you have and give to the poor, and you will have treasure in heaven" (see Mark 10:21). At first this sounds like a call to sacrifice, and in one sense it is. Indeed, in this man's heart the price proved too high for him to pay. He rejected Jesus' invitation.

But on closer examination, Jesus' words aren't a call to sacrifice as much as they're a call to satisfaction. Sure, Jesus beckoned the man to sell everything he has on earth, but in the next breath he promised the man everlasting treasure in eternity. When you stop and think about it, there's a tinge (or maybe much more than a tinge) of self-serving motivation for this man to care for the poor. It's as if Jesus was saying to him, "Give what you have to the poor; I'll give you something better." In the end Jesus wasn't calling this man away from treasure; Jesus was calling him to treasure. When we understand the passage in this way, we begin to realize that materialism isn't just sinful; it's stupid.

> *Truly, I say to you, there is no one who has left house or brothers or sisters or mother or father or children or lands, for my sake and for the gospel, who will not receive a hundredfold now in this time, houses and brothers and sisters and mothers and children and lands, with persecutions, and in the age to come eternal life.*
> Mark 10:29-30

Reading those verses, we can recognize a wise investment strategy. Anyone who can guarantee 10,000 percent interest is a good investor to work with.

Use the categories below to make a budget. Consider your income, expenses for necessities, what you'll save or invest, and what you'll give.

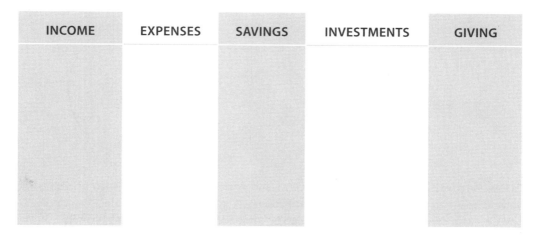

INCOME	EXPENSES	SAVINGS	INVESTMENTS	GIVING

Now go back and circle the nonessentials or luxuries you listed. Is Jesus asking you to change anything in order to store up treasure in heaven?

DAY 3
AS YOU LOVE YOURSELF

Scripture never teaches that care for the poor is a means to salvation. The Bible is clear, from cover to cover, that humble faith in divine grace is the only means to eternal salvation. But Scripture is also clear that God expects His people to care for those in need. As people created in the image of God, we're expected to reflect His loving character by caring for those He cares about.

Read Luke 10:25-28.

What two things did Jesus affirm as the most important commands for us to live by?

Love God with all your heart, ~~mind~~ soul & strength, mind
Love your neighbor as yourself

Fill in the following circles to indicate how completely you love God and your neighbor. Are you wholehearted in your love for God? In your love for neighbor?

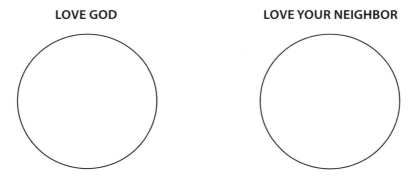

To love God with all of your heart, soul, mind, and strength is clear. It's all-encompassing and holistic. You're to love Him with everything you have and everything you are. Admittedly, however, this can feel a little abstract. It can become more of an idea than a lifestyle.

How would you explain loving God wholeheartedly in practical terms?

To love your neighbor as yourself is equally all-encompassing but has much more obvious practical implications. We're tempted to turn this into an abstract idea or emotion. But we can't escape or avoid the sobering truth of this command.

Imagine what you'd want someone to do for you if you lived in an impoverished village in a remote part of the world. What if you were born into a family in desperate circumstances? Wouldn't you want somebody to help you? Or what if your kids or the children in your church were dying of preventable diseases? What if half of your children were dying before their eighth birthdays? If it were us, or if these were our kids, or if this were families in our churches, we'd do something. Ignoring such urgent needs simply wouldn't be an option.

Yet this is exactly what so many of us in the Western church have done. We've insulated and isolated ourselves from the massive material poverty that surrounds us in the world. We've filled our lives and our churches with more comforts for ourselves while turning a blind eye and a deaf ear to abject poverty in others. We have a gaping hole in the way we see the world, and we need new sight. We need our eyes opened to the implications of the gospel for the way we live.

Ordinary, middle-class working Americans are extremely wealthy in a world surrounded by billions of extremely poor neighbors. And God has called us to love these neighbors—as ourselves.

WHO IS MY NEIGHBOR?

It's not enough to simply know the right answers. Truth leads to application; it becomes personal. After the expert in the law failed to stir up controversy or trip Jesus up with a theological question, the dialogue between them became more personal.

Read Luke 10:25-29.

What was the lawyer's motivation in verse 25? In verse 29?

Tried to trick Christ

Justify himself

How can questions and debates about God, the Bible, or supposedly spiritual interests actually be a way of postponing or denying a personal response?

We get into debates to prolong the conversation or time period so that we don't have to follow the Law of God.

Is there anything in your life—maybe even in relation to the poor, widows, or orphans—that you're using to justify inaction by asking more questions instead of meeting the needs of more people? If so, what?

Read Luke 10:30-37.

How was Jesus' response countercultural?

The so-called hero of this story was shocking in first-century Jewish context. A Samaritan shouldn't epitomize godly character, especially compared to a priest and a Levite. The person who fulfilled the law, loving God and loving his neighbor as himself, wasn't the person with a religious education or profession or the person born into the right family but the person who saw a need and met it. The Samaritan detoured from his own plans; invested his own time; energy, and resources; and went out of his way to help this person in need.

Jesus clearly responded with an emphasis on caring for the neighbors who are right next to us—whoever they may be. Believers and our churches are expected to love our neighbors.

Read Romans 15:26.

Underline the word *contribution*.   Koi-non-nia

The word Paul used for *contribution* was *koinonia,* which was the Greek word for *fellowship.* The word picture here is wonderful, for the fellowship fostered by this offering was a beautiful portrait of one part of the body of Christ saying to another, "We're with you. You aren't alone in your need."

Scripture is also clear that our first priority is to those in our own families (see 1 Tim. 5:8). However, the New Testament goes much further than simply calling Christians to care for members of their own physical families. In Christ, Christians have been adopted into an entirely new family that rises far above physical lineage. We no longer think only in terms of biological bloodline, for we've been united by an entirely different bloodline. In Christ, because of His shed blood for our sins, we've been brought together as brothers and sisters.

We haven't been put on this earth simply to preserve our genetic material. We've been put on this earth to portray a gospel message, and that gospel message crosses physical barriers and transcends biological bloodlines. This gospel truth has huge implications for the way followers of Christ think and speak about family.

What needs exist in your family?

What needs can you meet among the neighbors around you?

What needs can you meet among the members of your church?

What needs can you meet for the poor, widow, or orphan in your community and around the world?

Christ's command, coupled with the depth of poverty in the world and the reality of wealth in our lives, has huge implications for the way we live. When our eyes have been opened to conditions in the world around us, our ears must be open to the question God's Word asks of us:

If anyone has the world's goods and sees his brother in need, yet closes his heart against him, how does God's love abide in him?
1 John 3:17

To be clear, this is a specific reference to followers of Christ caring for other Christians in need. However, the command of Christ in Luke 10 to love our neighbors as ourselves surely includes care not just for the believing poor but also for the unbelieving poor. Such neighborly love is the natural overflow of men and women who know God. If the love of God is in our hearts, then it's not possible for us to ignore the poor in the world. The gospel compels Christians in a wealthy culture to action—selfless, sacrificial, costly, countercultural action—on behalf of the poor. For if we don't act in this way, then it may become clear that we were never Christians in the first place.

Prayerfully take an inventory of the blessings God has entrusted to you and determine how you can use them for the good of others and the glory of God.

What can you SHARE? Belongs:- Car, food, house

What can you SELL? Belongings :- Give to those in need

What can you SACRIFICE? - Time,

Bryant Park - Movie
5pm - 11pm

KEEP WORKING

From the beginning of history, work has been a mark of human dignity, a fundamental part of God's plan for men and women to steward the creation entrusted to them and to develop the culture around them.

Read Genesis 2:15.

What did God put man in the garden to do?

When we remember that this was before sin's entrance into the world, we realize that work is a good gift of God's grace. We often view work as a necessary evil, something we have to endure in order to make money, but this isn't how the Bible views work.

This issue is important because diligent work is one of the most obvious but often overlooked ways we provide for the poor. Sometimes people hear pleas to help the poor and immediately think, *Well, maybe I should quit this menial job I have in order to give more meaningful time to the poor.* I'm not saying that God won't lead some people to leave their professions for a particular purpose, but I do wonder whether this pattern of thinking exposes a fundamental flaw in our understanding of work. For in working hard on a daily basis, we lend our help to the development of a society that's able to sustain human life.

It isn't uncommon, especially among younger people, for someone to get convicted about a certain area of need in the world and decide that the obvious course of action is for them to stop wasting time in school or in a "secular job" and start doing something significant in the world. But could it be that God has actually led many to college and to the workplace for a reason? Could it be that rather than being a waste of time, it's actually a wise use of time to receive training in skills for a job that God will use in the future to accomplish His purpose in the world?

How have you been tempted to feel as if what you are doing in this season of your life isn't significant enough?

How can those responsibilities be blessings from God and opportunities to serve Him?

In addition, diligent work is the means by which we acquire necessities and even wealth. People who've read previous books I've written or who've heard me talk about possessions often ask, "David, are you saying it's wrong to make a lot of money?" The answer is always and unequivocally, "No. Make as much money as you can. Do it fairly and justly. Be a millionaire if the Lord provides you that opportunity!" People look surprised before hearing the clarification, "What matters most isn't how much you earn but what you do with what you earn."

God doesn't command the rich to stop making money; instead, He commands the rich to use their money on earth to store up treasure in eternity—exactly what you've studied this week.

As long as we're able, the gospel compels us to work diligently. We need to hear and heed this exhortation on polar ends of our cultural spectrum (and everywhere in between). On the one hand, work is seen as a necessary evil. On the other hand, our culture views work as the ultimate good—that which gives us our meaning and self-worth.

Where does your view of work fall on this cultural spectrum? Plot a point below.

├──┤

Necessary evil   Ultimate good

Where does your work ethic actually fall on this spectrum? Plot a second point above. Is it the same as what you say you believe about work? Explain any difference.

We live in a culture where many young people are prolonging adolescence into adulthood. Scores of males in their 20s and 30s, for example, are refusing to become men, playing video games instead of getting an education or a job, working part-time while leaning on their parents to pay their bills. Worst of all, some excuse their laziness with spiritual language, saying they're waiting to figure out what God wants them to do, all the while ignoring the glaring biblical reality that God wants them to work—to work hard for others' good and for His glory.

RETIREMENT?

This trend of avoiding work shouldn't surprise us in a culture that minimizes the value of work by magnifying the goal of retirement. Success, according to the standards of our society, is arriving at the place where you no longer work. Nowhere in Scripture do we see that God's design for productive minds and bodies is to perpetually lie on a beach, ride in a golf cart, or sit in a fishing boat. The entire concept of saving money so that we can live a life of luxury without working has no biblical foundation whatsoever. Retirement isn't a time to sit back and perpetually relax. It's a blessing to reach a point in life where you no longer have to work for a salary to meet the needs of your family and are free to serve in new ways for the glory of God!

I think of Jack, a man in his 60s who, when he was baptized in our church, plainly said, "My plan was to retire, buy a German sports car, and play tennis." But then he shared, "By God's grace, before I could put my plan into action, God intervened." Jack shared about how God had worked in his life, not just saving him from his sin but saving him from himself. Jack now uses his previous job skills to serve our church and the needy in our community, and he leads a ministry to orphans in Cameroon. "What a joy," he told our church, "to see the smiles of children as they push to get a seat on your lap and hold your hand because they have no earthly father and you're telling them about their Heavenly Father!" Then he concluded, "This is the plan God had for me, and the thrill and excitement of it far exceed retirement or any sports car."

Read Colossians 3:23-24.

What did Paul write to the church in Corinth about hard work and our reward?

Read Philippians 2:14-15.

What countercultural attitude should characterize the Christian life?

How does this teaching affect our view on work?

According to these verses, what's our motivation for a countercultural attitude?

HELPING OTHERS

This idea of work—if a person is able—works both ways. We work for the glory of God and for the good of others. We love our neighbors as ourselves, as we saw in day 3.

The worst thing we can do for the needy is to neglect them. But the second worst thing we can do is to subsidize them, helping people get through the day while ignoring how we can help people get through their lives.

Particularly in places like Proverbs and 1–2 Thessalonians, Scripture doesn't call us to rescue lazy people from poverty. Instead, Scripture calls us to serve and supplement the responsible. Even in a place like 1 Timothy 5, where Paul commanded the church to care for widows, he specifies "the widow who is really in need" (v. 5, NIV) and then went on to say that not every widow qualifies for church support. Consequently, we need to consider how to help those in need in ways that empower them to fulfill the purpose for which God created them instead of enabling them to miss that purpose.

Helping like this necessitates personal attention, consistent accountability, and long-term commitment. Giving to those in need isn't about sharing handouts; it's about sharing life. Helping those in need doesn't consist of throwing our money at something; it involves throwing our lives at someone, which is much, much harder to do.

What's your church doing to care for the poor, orphaned, and widowed?

What's your small group doing?

Are these temporary fixes? How can they become long-term solutions?

ONE OF THE PRIMARY WAYS WE HELP THE POOR

IS THROUGH DILIGENT WORK.

A GOSPEL RESPONSE TO ORPHANS, WIDOWS, & ISSUES OF POVERTY

Without question, our greatest wealth is found in the gospel itself, for God has saved us from our sins and has given us new life with Him. We are spiritually rich.

Read Ephesians 2:1-3.

What did Paul remind the church at Ephesus that they shared in common with everyone else in the world?

How does keeping this in mind create—

humility for ourselves?

hope for others?

Read Ephesians 2:4-9.

What do verses 4 and 7 describe in terms of true riches?

What did you do to earn God's favor?

Underline the phrase *so that* at the beginning of verse 7.

Why did God save us, changing our lives eternally?

Read 2 Corinthians 8:9.

Record 2 Corinthians 8:9 in the space provided below.

Underline the phrase *so that.*

God desires to show the world that He is "merciful and gracious, slow to anger, and abounding in steadfast love" (Ex. 34:6); that He "raises up the poor from the dust" and "lifts the needy from the ash heap" (1 Sam. 2:8); that He "executes justice for the oppressed" and "gives food to the hungry" (Ps. 146:7); that He's "a defense for the helpless" and "the needy in his distress" (Isa. 25:4, NASB). These characteristics of God are ultimately revealed in Christ, who came "to proclaim good news to the poor" and "to set at liberty those who are oppressed" (Luke 4:18).

Once we see this portrait of God in Christ, we realize that caring for the poor isn't just necessary evidence of faith in Him; it's the natural (or supernatural) overflow of faith in Him. Doesn't it make sense that those of us who love God as our Father would subsequently live as "imitators of God, as beloved children," walking "in love, as Christ loved us and gave himself up for us" (Eph. 5:1-2)? As people whom Christ has cared for sacrificially in our poverty, aren't we compelled to care for others selflessly in their poverty?

Even more, as materially wealthy men and women in a world of urgent spiritual and physical need, don't we want to reflect the majesty of our God in mercy toward the poor?

GLORY, NOT GUILT

Christians in our culture shouldn't care for the poor because we feel obligated—burdened by a low-grade sense of guilt when we look at the world. Sure, when we realize that nearly 19,000 children die each day of preventable diseases and recognize that we're some of the most affluent people ever to walk on the planet, our eyes are opened. But simple guilt in the face of global statistics doesn't produce sustainable obedience to God's commands. We may change our ways for a short time based on guilt, but it won't last.

Instead, real, authentic, sustainable care for the poor will happen only when any low-grade sense of guilt is conquered by a high-grade sense of gospel. For in the gospel—the good news of God's great love in Christ—Christians are compelled to a willing, joyful, urgent, faith-driven, grace-saturated, God-glorifying work on behalf of the poor. We don't care for the poor because of some superficial sense that we *have* to but because of a supernatural compulsion that causes us to *want* to.

Now to be clear, this "want to" doesn't necessarily happen overnight. Growth in the Christian life often begins with obedience to the commands of Christ even when acute desire isn't present. However, over the course of obedience, followers of Christ learn to trust that the ways of Christ are indeed good. As we care for the poor over time, what may have initially been obedience out of duty ("have to") inevitably becomes obedience out of delight ("want to").

> In your own experience, when has an act of duty and obedience turned into an act of joy and desire?

> When have you experienced failure in your continued commitment to do something solely out of guilt?

> How is a desire to see God glorified more compelling and sustainable than being motivated by guilt?

Heed this caution. While we care for the poor, we'll be tempted to forget the gospel along the way, especially when the culture around us applauds or criticizes our efforts. Unfortunately, Christian history is littered with stories of men and women who passionately worked on behalf of the poor but subtly loosened their grip on the gospel. Appropriately liberal concern for the needs of the world has often led to dangerously liberal approaches to the truth of God's Word, causing many Christians who believe the Bible today to be cautious about social action.

But we mustn't be cautious with something about which God is so clear. From cover to cover in Scripture, we don't read of a God who's tentative toward the poor. Instead, God is extravagant in His eagerness to hear, help, defend, and demonstrate His compassion to them. Therefore, the people of God must be nothing less. Yes, we must heed the warnings of history, but in our supposed efforts to guard the gospel, we run the dangerous risk of disobeying our God.

If this is an area of your life where you've been disobedient to the commands of God's Word by neglecting the poor, the gospel is still good news. For God forgives this sin too, and by His Spirit He can and will enable you to walk in a new path of sacrificial love for your neighbor in need.

YOUR RESPONSE

So what does such sacrificial love look like? What does the gospel compel us to do with our wealth in a world of poverty? We've seen this week that the gospel calls us to live simply, give sacrificially, help constructively, invest eternally, and work diligently.

Gospel realization creates gospel motivation to care for orphans and widows. For we aren't rescuers giving our lives and families to save orphans and widows in need; instead, we're the rescued whose lives have been transformed at our deepest point of need. So now it just makes sense that men and women who've been captivated by the mystery of God's mercy might be compelled to give themselves to the ministry of God's mercy—compelled to care for the orphan and the widow in our churches and around our world through a variety of different means.

> How does the gospel shape what you believe about wealth and poverty? Write a simple statement of your views on material possessions.

How does the gospel shape what you believe about caring for orphans and widows? Write a simple statement of what you believe God is telling you.

How do conversations about wealth, poverty, widows, and/or orphans open doors to share the gospel? Write a simple statement explaining how this particular issue is rooted in a foundational understanding of the gospel and our relationship with God.

Identify a specific time when you've been in a conversation or an incident related to issues of wealth, poverty, widows, or orphans. Describe the conversation and your perceived outcome.

Following this study, would you say or do anything differently?   YES   NO
How will you approach this issue in the future?

HUMAN LIFE

WELCOME EVERYONE TO THE THIRD GROUP DISCUSSION OF *COUNTER CULTURE*.

What was most helpful, encouraging, or challenging in your study of week 2?

What specific examples of issues related to human life have you seen in the news or on social media lately, such as abortion, pornography, and sexual exploitation? Share a recent news story related to human life.

To prepare to view the DVD segment, read aloud Genesis 1:26-28,31.

God said, "Let us make man in our image, after our likeness. And let them have dominion over the fish of the sea and over the birds of the heavens and over the livestock and over all the earth and over every creeping thing that creeps on the earth."

> *God created man in his own image,*
> > *in the image of God he created him;*
> > *male and female he created them.*

And God blessed them. And God said to them, "Be fruitful and multiply and fill the earth and subdue it, and have dominion over the fish of the sea and over the birds of the heavens and over every living thing that moves on the earth." And God saw everything that he had made, and behold, it was very good. And there was evening and there was morning, the sixth day.
Genesis 1:26-28,31

COMPLETE THE VIEWER GUIDE BELOW AS YOU WATCH DVD SESSION 3.

THE NATURE OF GOD

He is the supreme _____, the sovereign _____, the righteous _____, and the merciful _____.

THE NATURE OF LIFE

1. We are created in the _____ of God.

   • We are a unique _____ of God, utterly _____ on God, and ultimately _____ to God.

2. We are created for the _Purpose_ of God.

   • Created to enjoy a _realtionshyp_ with God, to _rule_ over all creation, and to _reproduce_ God's glory to the ends of the earth

THE NATURE OF SIN

1. The _Core_ of sin

   • Rejecting God's _Word_: Whose voice will we listen to?

   • Spurning God's _Authority_: Who will rule our hearts?

   • Denying God's _Character_: Whom will we trust and obey?

2. The _Conflict_ brought about by sin

   • Conflict between man and _God_, between man and _woman_, and between man and _creation_

3. The _Consequences_ of sin

   • Immediate _Spiritual_ death and eventual _physical_ death

THE NEED FOR SALVATION

1. Genesis 1–11 gives us glimpses of _grace_: the promise of _Christ_

2. Genesis 1–11 compels us to counter _culture_.

   • We oppose abortion because it destroys the _beauty_ of human life, work to end slavery because it denies the _equality_ of human life, and fight pornography because it denigrates the _dignity_ of human life.

Video sessions available for purchase at *www.lifeway.com/counterculture*

DISCUSS THE DVD SEGMENT WITH YOUR GROUP, USING THE QUESTIONS BELOW.

What was most helpful, encouraging, or challenging in this session? Why?

How does seeing God as Creator change our perspective on life? God as King? Judge? Savior?

How does being a unique reflection of God affect the way you view your own life?

How does acknowledging that all people are created in the image of God affect your view of issues related to human life like abortion? Sex trafficking? Sexual exploitation? Pornography?

David said, "The ultimate lie is that there are not eternal consequences for your sins." Explain what this means.

In Genesis 3 we see that sin first entered the world when God's words were questioned. In what ways do you question what God has said? Where does our culture tempt us to doubt God's good design and authority? How is blame still shifted?

How does the gospel compel action related to issues of human life?

How do issues of human life open a door to conversations about the gospel? Give examples of statements that relate the gospel to abortion, sexual exploitation, or pornography.

THIS WEEK
Memorize Genesis 1:27 and pray that God will break your heart over the objectification of, abuse of, and disregard for human life in the womb and in the world. Identify practical steps to guard yourself against pornography and sexually explicit content.

READ week 3 and complete the activities before the next group experience.
READ chapters 3 and 5 in the book *Counter Culture* by David Platt (Tyndale, 2015).

HUMAN LIFE

> *God created man in his own image,*
> *in the image of God he created him;*
> *male and female he created them.*
> Genesis 1:27

"All the details differ, but the essential element in the astronomical and biblical accounts of Genesis is the same. … This is an exceedingly strange development, unexpected by all but the theologians. They have always accepted the word of the Bible: In the beginning God created heaven and earth. … The development is unexpected because science has had such extraordinary success in tracing the chain of cause and effect backward in time. … At this moment it seems as though science will never be able to raise the curtain on the mystery of creation. For the scientist who has lived by his faith in the power of reason, the story ends like a bad dream. He has scaled the mountains of ignorance; he is about to conquer the highest peak; as he pulls himself over the final rock, he is greeted by a band of theologians who have been sitting there for centuries."[1]

Robert Jastrow

This week our focus moves from loving our neighbor in terms of poverty and possessions to a more holistic view of human life. How are the issues of abortion, pornography, and sex slavery related, and how does the truth of the gospel change the way we live in light of these tragedies?

1. Robert Jastrow, *God and the Astronomers* (Readers Library, 1992), 14, 106–7.

DAY 1
THE IMAGE OF GOD

We've already seen that it's increasingly unpopular to believe in God, especially a God who's our personal Creator.

But a foundational belief in God as Creator and humans as His creation shapes our view of all human life. Not only are we created by God, but we are also created uniquely—distinct from everything else in His creation. We aren't merely a more sophisticated animal at the top of the food chain. We're a unique creation. See it here in Genesis 1.

Read Genesis 1:11-12,20-25.

Circle the word *kind* when it appears in these verses. What does *kind* refer to in each of these verses? Why is this a significant detail?

This is the same word used again later in the story of Noah, as the animals were gathered according to their kind (see Gen. 6:20; 7:14).

Also pay attention to another pattern that's being established. Notice that each act of creation begins with "God said" and concludes with "[it] was good." What does this pattern teach us about God and His creation?

Over and over throughout the creation narrative, God spoke with authority to His creation. Up to this point God had spoken for six days, "Let there be this. Let there be that." And it was so. And it was good. Every time. The expression of His will is always good. By the sheer power of His voice, He created everything up to this point. And He saw that it was good.

Don't miss that second part. First, it was all established by His power and authority. Second, He declared it to be good. This is a deeply personal point. This isn't an abstract concept or a random detail. The created order, all of God's design, is good. He takes delight in His creation. God isn't indifferent. Everything was the exact expression of His desire. He spoke it all into being.

Then there's a sudden and significant change in the pattern. The pattern that had built up over the six days of creation highlights the distinction and the break in the rhythm. This should grab our attention and cause us to ask, "Why the change?" God had been speaking to creation and creating things according to their kind. Then see what He did.

Read Genesis 1:26-31.

Instead of saying things like "let the earth" and "let the waters," what did God say when creating humankind? Instead of speaking to creation, to whom was He speaking?

Rather than man and woman being created according to any other kind, what likeness did they share? Why is this significant?

How were man and woman further set apart with a distinct position among the created order?

What's God's declaration following the conclusion of creation on this sixth day?

Man isn't just a more sophisticated or better adapted creature. We aren't distinct among other organisms—plants and animals—by a matter of degree. Humans—men and women—are uniquely created in the image of God. We aren't God. We aren't exactly like Him. Obviously, we're unable to speak physical matter and living beings into existence, for starters. But we share a special relationship with Him that no other created being experiences in all His good creation.

Look at the close relationship between God and humankind described in Genesis 2. This parallel account focuses on the personal nature of God in creation.

Read Genesis 2:7.

How was God more intimately involved in the creation of man than simply speaking him into existence?

Read Genesis 2:21-22.

How was God more intimately involved in the creation of woman than simply speaking her into existence?

Notice that the personal name of God is also included in Genesis 2. He isn't simply God. He's the LORD God. He's Yahweh, the God who makes Himself known to His people throughout biblical history. The same God who makes Himself known desires a personal relationship with you—someone created in His image.

A similar picture is seen in the New Testament as well. Last week you read what Paul wrote to the church in Ephesus (see Eph. 2:1-9): that by the gift of God He has blessed His children abundantly, in His rich mercy. Our Heavenly Father chose to give us life. This is the good news of the gospel. And look at the next declaration that Paul made in Ephesians.

Read Ephesians 2:10.

Notice the word *workmanship*.

The word translated *workmanship* here can also read *handiwork, creation,* or *masterpiece.* Our word *poem* comes from this same Greek word.

How does this idea of being God's unique creation—His masterpiece, handiwork, or even poem—affect the way you view yourself?

What does being God's workmanship say about His care for every detail in your life?

How does knowing that other people are also His workmanship, created in God's image in Christ Jesus for good works that He has prepared, shape your view of human life?

Notice that, as in the creation account in Genesis, Paul said we're created as a unique and good expression of God. What other language in this verse paints a picture similar to God's original design for humanity in the garden of Eden?

Men and women are unique among all creation. We're created in the image of God. This isn't simply a story we tell children about how the world began and where people originated. This is a foundational truth that shapes our view of life itself. Recognizing that men and women are created in the image of God has radical implications for practically every issue that our culture debates. When we embrace this simple yet profound truth, seemingly complicated or confusing issues become clear. They're no longer issues, really. We'll look more specifically at how this relates to cultural issues in the days and weeks to come. For now, let your heart be glad. Be in awe. Join the psalmist in marveling at the wonder of all God's creation and the fact that He's chosen not only to create us but also to care for us in a uniquely personal way.

Read Psalm 8.

Record a prayer thanking God for creating and caring for you personally.

COVENANT

Even though men and women were created in the image of God, unique from and superior to all other creation, it didn't take long for things to unravel.

We saw yesterday that in the beginning, Adam and Eve were created in the image and likeness of God. However, in the first week of the study, we also saw that they turned right around and questioned God, doubted His goodness, denied His authority, and sinned against Him. The result was death and a broken relationship with God.

God would have been perfectly just and fair to end the human story right there. What arrogance! What incredible sin, to seek life apart from our Creator! All creation had obeyed the command of God. Light came into existence and separated from darkness. The entire natural design was established at the very word of God; the simple expression of His will brought forth everything out of nothing. Let the magnitude of this reality sink in.

In the Book of Job we see a vivid description of the intricate details of God's design. We also see the infinite disparity between the understanding and power of our Creator compared to that of humankind, the pinnacle of His creation.

Read Job 38:4-38; 40:1-4.

Summarize God's response to Job's question.

Summarize Job's response after being reminded of God's authority.

The poetic response of God to Job's question is both awesome and humbling. Everything in creation bows to the will of God. Only man talks back and questions Him. Only humanity, the very creation made in the image and likeness of the Creator, has the audacity to doubt, deny, and disobey the Word of God. It's important to pause and feel the weight of this reality. Only when we begin to see the glorious goodness of our Creator do we begin to recognize the gravity of our sin against Him. What foolishness to assume, even for an instant, that we could possibly know or do better for ourselves than the plans and purposes God has put in place.

This has been true since the very first man and woman. And just as God had warned, death immediately followed sin. And then in the verses and chapters that follow, we see the presence of hope in the form of a promise. It's God's faithfulness amid another extremely dark scene— the flooding of the world as God brought judgment on creation. In Genesis 6 we see two words for the first time in Scripture: *grace* and *covenant*.

> *The L*ord *saw that the wickedness of man was great in the earth, and that every intention of the thoughts of his heart was only evil continually. And the L*ord *regretted that he had made man on the earth, and it grieved him to his heart. So the L*ord *said, "I will blot out man whom I have created from the face of the land, man and animals and creeping things and birds of the heavens, for I am sorry that I have made them." But Noah found favor in the eyes of the L*ord.
> Genesis 6:5-8

Underline the phrase *found favor in the eyes of the L*ord. **Circle or highlight the word** *favor.*

The wording in verse 8 is literally "received grace in the eyes of the LORD." The Hebrew word translated here as *favor* is most often translated as *grace.*

Write a simple definition of the word *grace.* **(See Eph. 2:8 if you need a reminder.)**

Why is it important to note that grace is a vital part of the story of Noah?

Read Genesis 6:11-13.

What did God say was the reason for judging the world?

According to verse 12, who was responsible for sin?

What does the word *corrupt* imply about God's design and man's freedom?

Read Genesis 6:18-22.

Circle or highlight the word *covenant*.

God spoke to Noah and gave him a promise of how He was going to preserve him. It's the first time we see the word *covenant* in the Bible. And God revealed how He was going to provide for Noah and his family and save them from the coming judgment.

God provided specific instructions on how Noah would be saved. Precise measurements were given, and certain materials were specified. Noah responded in faithful obedience.

How does the story of Noah demonstrate God's sovereignty?

How does the story of Noah demonstrate man's responsibility?

Verse 18 introduces the concept of *covenant*. What does that word mean? It depicts a loving commitment God has toward His people. He was saying, "I'm going to provide for you amid a world that deserves My judgment. I'm going to show grace. I'm going to initiate My relationship with sinners." That's what God did with Noah and his family.

This huge glimpse of grace coming through a covenant sets the stage for the rest of the story line of Scripture. Praise God that He hasn't left us alone in our sin, when every single one of us has rebelled against Him. We've questioned His Word. We've spurned His authority. We've doubted and denied His character. We're separated from Him in our sin, having rebelled against Him. We're dead without Him.

But by His grace we're saved. By His faithfulness God doesn't close the book on human history. He isn't done with the story. He shows grace. He establishes a covenant. He still has good works prepared for men and women, created in His image, to do.

See this glorious picture as Noah and his family exit the ark after God's judgment on the earth through the flood. Notice the language God used to speak to Noah.

Read Genesis 9:1-9.

What similarities exist between Genesis 9:1-9 and Genesis 1:26-31? What differences?

What does this say about God's faithfulness, despite our sin?

What warning did God give about human life (see Gen. 9:6)?

What reason did God give for the seriousness of His command about human life?

Consider the fact that, in the midst of a sinful culture, Noah heard the voice of God and did exactly as God said. He went completely against the grain of society, building an ark that surely seemed ridiculous to everyone around him. Ask yourself, *Am I willing to trust God, no matter how crazy it may look to the world?* And if so, consider, *Would I hear God in order to obey Him? Am I even listening?* The answer to those questions had life-changing, world-changing implications for Noah. The same is true for you—and for those around you—today.

ABORTION

Human life is a matter of God's holiness and His love. From the opening pages of Scripture, we've seen man and woman created in the image of God and corrupt people going their own way, sinning against Him. We've also seen a loving Creator and Savior extending grace and establishing a covenant—a promise of hope in a seemingly hopeless world.

Abortion isn't just an issue here in the United States. Throughout the world over 42 million abortions occur every year.[1] That's, at minimum, 115,000 abortions every single day. This is a tragedy of epic proportions. Every single day 115,000 human lives are lost.

But the world doesn't blink an eye. Not only does our culture fail to see this overwhelming death toll as a tragedy. It's also seen as a choice. As a freedom. As a right. How corrupt have we become as a society, to borrow language from the story of Noah, that positive language has been wrapped around such a negative reality?

What was the last major news story involving a natural disaster or tragedy that cost innocent people their lives?

You may remember exactly where you were when you heard the news of a particular disaster or tragedy. We rightly mourn the loss of human life as we're awakened to the fragility of human life. Yet the reality is that 115,000 humans are being systematically executed every single day. They aren't lost accidentally or naturally. Innocent babies are intentionally, purposefully, and willfully being murdered. Right now. As you read this.

It's almost too much even to fathom. The numbers can be so overwhelming that they no longer seem real. Let's do the math for the sake of seeing each and every individual person.

115,000 abortions every day / 24 hours every day = _____ abortions every hour.

_____ abortions every hour / 60 minutes = _____ abortions every minute.

_____ abortions every minute / 60 seconds = _____ abortions every second.

To be clear, when we say "abortions," we mean human beings killed in the womb.

Snap your finger at one-second intervals and count, "1, 2, 3, 4 ... ," and you can't keep up with the rate at which innocent human lives are being taken. More than one human life is taken by abortion every second. And if you're able to easily dismiss these numbers as anything other than representing human lives around the world and a crisis unlike any the world has ever known, then ask yourself, *What value do you place on human life—little boys and girls who are created in the image of God?*

We know for sure the value God places on every human life.

Read Matthew 10:29-31.

What name did Jesus use to refer to God? What does this word reveal about a person's relationship with God?

What did Jesus say about every minute detail regarding human life?

Based on Jesus' illustration, at what point is a life too small or insignificant in the eyes of our Heavenly Father?

Read Psalm 127:3.

Our culture views children as a choice. Often they're even seen as a burden, an accident, or an inconvenience. How does Scripture describe children?

If you or anyone at this point could question whether the statistics on the previous page are horrific or whether the love and care of our Father apply in these instances, the underlying question is undoubtedly whether that which is in the womb is human.

This is ultimately the only real point for any debate or discussion about abortion. The key question we all must answer—and the question that determines how we view abortion—is this: What's contained in the womb? Is it a person? Or is it merely an embryo, a fetus? Virtually every other question and every single argument in the abortion controversy comes back to this question. What or who is in the womb? And once this question is answered, everything else comes into perspective. Answer the question for yourself.

Is the unborn a person?   YES   NO

If the unborn isn't a person, then no justification for abortion is even necessary. If the unborn is a person, then no justification for abortion is ever adequate.

What arguments have you heard (or given) in support of abortion (or "choice")?

Many people say, "Abortion is such a complex issue, and there just aren't any easy answers." But if that which is in the womb is a person, then even if someone is pro-abortion or pro-choice for any number of reasons, all of their reasoning falls apart. Regardless of where you currently stand on the abortion issue, imagine for a moment that the unborn is a person formed and created by God Himself. If this is true, then think through the primary arguments for abortion.

Read Psalm 139:13-16.

What does this Scripture say about the unborn in the womb?

How do you see the foundational truth of God as Creator in this Scripture?

How does this Scripture relate to what you studied in day 1 about God's workmanship (see Eph. 2:10)?

These verses are even more stunning when we realize that the psalmist came to his conclusions without knowing the details we know today about a baby's development. This work of creation evokes awe and amazement. One of the wonderful things about Psalm 139 is the glimpse we get into how God relates to a child in the womb. He's intimately involved in the life of that baby from the moment of conception—and even before that!

God told Jeremiah, "Before I formed you in the womb, I knew you; before you were born I sanctified you" (Jer. 1:5, NKJV). The psalmist said to God, "You are He who took Me out of the womb. … From My mother's womb You have been My God" (Ps. 22:9-10, NKJV). Scripture says God calls, names, and blesses children while they're still in the womb (see Isa. 49:1; Luke 1:15; Gal. 1:15). The Bible even describes a baby leaping with joy in the womb (see Luke 1:39-44)!

God reminds us in His Word that though an unborn baby is visibly hidden from us, he or she isn't hidden from Him. God sees children in wombs all across the world right now, and He's personally and intimately forming, fashioning, knitting, creating, nurturing, shaping, and crafting them in wonderful ways (see Job 31:15).

The hope is that every follower of Christ and every church leader will see how the gospel comes to bear on abortion. And in so doing, we'll be compelled, not by way of party politics but by way of gospel passion, to speak clearly and stand boldly against abortion, both in our country and around the world.

So what about those who've participated in abortion? How do we cope personally or minister to those who've suffered such a tragedy? Is abortion a sin? Absolutely. Do we all need a Savior? Absolutely. Is God's grace sufficient for us all? Absolutely, yes. In day 5 we'll focus on how God forgives and restores us. For now know that hope and healing are available in Jesus.

> *He does not deal with us according to our sins,*
> *nor repay us according to our iniquities.*
> *For as high as the heavens are above the earth,*
> *so great is his steadfast love toward those who fear him;*
> *as far as the east is from the west,*
> *so far does he remove our transgressions from us.*
> *As a father shows compassion to his children,*
> *so the LORD shows compassion to those who fear him.*
> *For he knows our frame;*
> *he remembers that we are dust.*
> Psalm 103:10-14

1. Susan A. Cohen, "Facts and Consequences: Legality, Incidence and Safety of Abortion Worldwide," *Guttmacher Policy Review*, Fall 2009, vol. 12, no. 4 [online, cited 26 November 2014]. Available from the Internet: *www.guttmacher.org*.

DAY 4

PORNOGRAPHY & SEX SLAVERY

Many of us may not realize the severity of sex trafficking in the world around us, or perhaps we didn't until recently. For a long time the idea of slavery seemed like a bad dream, a terrible blot on the pages of human history. But exploiting human beings for personal gain isn't just a problem from our past. It's an everyday reality, a living nightmare from which more than 27 million men, women, boys, and girls never wake up to escape.[1]

Do you realize there are more slaves in the world right now, as you read this, than the total number who were seized from Africa in four centuries of the Trans-Atlantic Slave Trade? More people live in slavery today than at any other time in world history. Millions are being bought, sold, and exploited for sex in what has become one of the fastest-growing industries on earth.

Like abortion and other issues, until these numbers become human to you, they'll be easy to ignore. They'll simply be statistics, numbers, or issues. We must pray that God opens our eyes to see men and women created in the image of God, souls in need of earthly and eternal salvation, as our brothers and sisters in Christ. The gospel demands action. We can't be silent.

When were you first exposed to the reality of sexual exploitation, sexual slavery, or pornography?

In what ways does our culture treat men and women like commodities to be consumed or used to meet personal desires?

Think back to week 1's study on idolatry. In what ways does our culture idolize sex?

American culture is saturated in the worship of sex, which has led to a widespread devaluation of women. This is apparent not only in our prostitution industry but also in our pornography industry, and it's evident not only in the culture around us but also in the churches among us. Surveys consistently show that more than half of men and increasing numbers of women in churches actively view pornography. Shockingly, statistics are similar for the pastors who lead these churches.[2]

Our culture jokes about or honestly embraces the perspective that it's OK to look but not to touch (though many would justify any behavior). Some go so far as to encourage indulgent thoughts of lust or anger in the belief that giving an outlet to such desires is healthy and preferable to acting on them toward others. Though few would dare to joke about sex slavery, our culture makes frequent jokes about pornography. Just as bad, our culture openly exploits men and women as objects of sexual desire in advertising and entertainment.

Explain the cultural truism "You can look, but you can't touch."

What other rationale have you heard in our culture defending pornography or sexually explicit materials?

Now let's see what the Bible says.

Read Matthew 5:27-30.

What did Jesus say about lustful thoughts?

This isn't just Jesus using hyperbole. Yes, He exaggerated to make a point. Please don't pluck out your eye or cut off your hand. But His point about lust is serious. If lustful thoughts consume your heart and mind, do whatever you have to do to turn your heart and mind back to reverence for God.

How is any form of objectification—even subtle forms in advertising and popular entertainment and fashion—dehumanizing and therefore hateful?

Read 1 John 3:15.

What does this Scripture say about the seriousness of our so-called private thoughts and secret desires—even those we don't act on?

How do Jesus and John counter culture in equating thoughts and actions?

Pornography is obviously a severe problem on multiple levels, but don't miss its connection to sex trafficking. Research continually demonstrates that at least a third of victims trafficked for sex are used in the production of pornography. Men and women who indulge in pornography are themselves creating the demand for the sex-trafficking industry. Yet the cycle is even more vicious than that. For the more people watch pornography, the more they desire sexual fulfillment through prostitution. Pornography thus feeds prostitution, thereby increasing the demand for sex trafficking.

Do we realize what we're doing? Every time someone views pornography, we're contributing to a cycle of sex slavery from the privacy of our own computers, phones, and media devices. We're fueling an industry that enslaves people for sex in order to satisfy selfish pleasure.

Do we see the depth of irony here? A quick survey of the college landscape in our culture reveals zealous activism on behalf of slaves around the world. Students watch documentaries, listen to speakers, hold charity walks and runs, and raise money to help trafficking victims. Meanwhile, almost 90 percent of college males and over 30 percent of college females are viewing porn in their dorms, apartments, and on their phones.[3] And this isn't limited to secular campuses or non-Christian activists. According to a recent study of evangelical Christian colleges, nearly 80 percent of male undergraduate students at these colleges have viewed Internet pornography in the past year, and more than 60 percent view it every week.[4] The hypocrisy is staggering, and the conclusion is clear.

Pornography is slavery. It enslaves the viewer with addictive effects on the brain. Eventually, the so-called harmless viewing of pornography is no longer sufficient for satisfying the insatiable desires of men and women. They seek other ways to feed their cravings, becoming more and more involved in a vicious cycle of dehumanizing behavior.

Any and every time a man or a woman indulges in pornography, he or she denies the precious gospel truth that every man and woman possesses inherent dignity, not to be solicited and sold for sex but to be valued and treasured as excellent in the eyes of God. People aren't inferior objects to be used and abused for selfish, sexual, sensual pleasure; they're equal image bearers of the God who loves and cares for them. We may scoff at how pre–Civil War churchgoers justified slaves in their backyards, but aren't we dangerously like them when we participate in pornography (and promote the sex slavery to which it's inextricably tied) in our own homes and from our own phones?

Read James 4:1-10.

What warning did James offer about the secret desires of our heart spilling out into our behavior?

What did James instruct as the only appropriate response to sinful desires and the goodness of the gospel?

Read Titus 3:3-8.

What humbling reminder and encouragement are offered in these verses?

1. "The State Department 2013 Trafficking in Persons Report," U.S. Department of State [online], 11 July 11 2013 [cited 26 November 2014]. Available from the Internet: www.state.gov.

2. "Staggering Statistics," MindArmor Training Tools [online, cited 3 December 2014]. Available from the Internet: www.mind-armor.com/staggering-statistics.

3. Angela Lu, "Connecting the dots between sex trafficking and pornography," World [online], 10 June 2013 [cited 1 December 2014]. Available from the Internet: www.worldmag.com/2013/06/connecting_the_dots_between_sex_trafficking_and_pornography.

4. Paul Olaf Chelsen, "An Examination of Internet Pornography Usage Among Male Students at Evangelical Christian Colleges," Loyola University Chicago, 2011 dissertation [online, cited 1 December 2014]. Available from the Internet: http://ecommons.luc.edu/luc_diss/150.

DAY 5
A GOSPEL RESPONSE TO
ISSUES OF HUMAN LIFE

Remember: God is not only the Judge of sin but also the Savior of sinners.

Chances are, according to statistics, that you've been personally affected by the sins of either abortion or pornography. If not, you know somebody who has. For certain, you've been exposed to forms of exploitation and the dehumanization of others who are created in the image of God. No matter how extreme or subtle your exposure or involvement may seem, any objectification of another human being is sin against both them and their Creator.

But God's forgiveness is available. You saw this week that God removes the sins of those who love Him, "as far as the east is from the west" (Ps. 103:11-12). Yes, sin separates us from God. But it doesn't have to come between us forever.

Read Isaiah 43:25.

Sins such as abortion and pornography haunt the mind. What does this verse say about this seemingly inescapable memory of sin?

What does it mean that God forgives your sin for His sake?

Read 1 John 1:8-9.

What's necessary to experience the freedom of God's forgiveness?

If you've been enslaved to the memory of abortion or the addiction to pornography, what step do you need to take right now?

The good news of the gospel is that when we turn from our sin and trust in Christ, we find that He's paid the price for any part we've ever played in sins against others, and because of His cross, we're entirely forgiven.

How is abortion a sin against God and people created in His image?

How is pornography a sin against God and people created in His image?

God not only forgives entirely but also heals deeply. God doesn't desire for you or anyone else to live with the pain of regret. It's altogether right to hate sin in your history. The pain of past sin is often a powerful deterrent to future sin, but don't let it rob you of the peace God has designed for you in the present.

Read Luke 7:36-39.

What's the religious person's response to the sinful woman?

How does the church (or perhaps how do you and your friends) resemble the Pharisee on the issue of human life?

Read Luke 7:40-46.

Take a moment to consider the size of your debt—your desperate need for grace.

What hope does Jesus' response offer to those burdened by shame?

What conviction does it offer in terms of religious and moral pride?

Read Luke 7:47-50.

What did Jesus ultimately say to the woman who'd lived an immoral lifestyle?

God desires that peace to be yours today through repentance and faith. He forgives entirely, He heals deeply, and He restores completely. To all who trust in Christ, remember this: in Christ you're not guilty, and there's no condemnation for you. You don't walk around with a scarlet A on your chest, for God doesn't look at you and see the guilt of abortion. Instead, He looks at you and sees the righteousness of Christ. He doesn't forever hold over your head the countless times you've viewed pornography or objectified others in any way. God restores, and He redeems. God has a track record of working all things, including evil things, ultimately for good.

The more than 27 million men, women, and children enslaved at this very moment need a Savior who comes to them, like a shepherd who leaves 99 sheep to search for the 1, like a woman who turns her house upside down looking for a lost coin, and like a father who goes sprinting after a wayward son (see Luke 15). In their endless feelings of filth, they need a Savior who will look at them with compassionate eyes and say, "I will make you clean" (see Luke 5:12-14). With hopeless feelings of shame, they need a Savior who will restore their honor on this earth and renew their hope for all eternity.

This is the same Savior traffickers need as well. The men and women behind the trafficking industry need to see the severe nature of their sin and God's coming judgment on that sin. At the same time, they need to see the gracious sacrifice of God to ransom their souls. They need a Savior who will forgive their sins and transform their lives so that they'll no longer take advantage of helpless victims but instead advocate for them. Only the power of the gospel can bring about this kind of change in evil hearts. And the same can be said for the men and women who use these precious souls in prostitution and watch them in pornography.

When it comes down to it, you need this Savior. They need this Savior. We all need God, in His mercy, to serve us with His salvation. We all need Him to change us from the inside out so that we can follow Him as the only Lord over all and so that we can love the people around us, recognizing the dignity He has bestowed on them. When this gospel changes our lives, it changes the way we relate to the people around us.

For Christians, it's the portrait of Christ in the gospel that compels us to fight for the end of slavery and any form of exploitation and objectification in the world. We can't be silent, and we mustn't be still. We don't have that choice. In the midst of our praying, giving, and working, we're compelled to proclaim Christ, who alone has the ability to bring complete freedom. We're compelled to fight in all these ways with the truth of the gospel on our minds, the power of the gospel in our hearts, and the love of the gospel in our hands.

How does the gospel shape what you believe about abortion? Record a simple statement of what you believe.

How does the gospel shape what you believe about sexual exploitation in any form—sex slavery, prostitution, and pornography? Record a simple statement of what you believe.

How do conversations about abortion open opportunities to share the gospel? Record a simple statement explaining how this particular issue is rooted in a foundational understanding of the gospel and our relationship with God.

How can the issues of pornography and sexual slavery open opportunities to share the gospel? Record a simple statement explaining how these particular issues are rooted in a foundational understanding of the gospel and our relationship with God.

Identify a specific time when you've been in a conversation or incident related to issues of abortion, pornography, or sexual exploitation. Describe the conversation and your perceived outcome.

Following this study, would you say or do anything differently?   YES   NO
How will you approach this issue in the future?

GOD DESIRES PEACE TO BE YOURS TODAY

THROUGH REPENTANCE AND FAITH.

WEEK 4
SEXUALITY

WELCOME TO THIS FOURTH GROUP DISCUSSION OF *COUNTER CULTURE*.

What was most helpful, encouraging, or challenging in your study of week 3?

What issues of sexuality, gender, or marriage have you seen in the news lately? Share a recent news story related to sexuality, gender, and marriage.

To prepare to view the DVD segment, read aloud Genesis 2:21-25.

The LORD God caused a deep sleep to fall upon the man, and while he slept took one of his ribs and closed up its place with flesh. And the rib that the LORD God had taken from the man he made into a woman and brought her to the man. Then the man said,

>   *"This at last is bone of my bones*
>
>>   *and flesh of my flesh;*
>
>   *she shall be called Woman,*
>
>>   *because she was taken out of Man."*

Therefore a man shall leave his father and his mother and hold fast to his wife, and they shall become one flesh. And the man and his wife were both naked and were not ashamed.
Genesis 2:21-25

COMPLETE THE VIEWER GUIDE BELOW AS YOU WATCH DVD SESSION 4.

THREE TRUTHS ABOUT MANHOOD AND WOMANHOOD

1. God created men and women with _____ dignity.

2. God created men and women with _____ roles.

   • Man and woman _____ each other.

   • Man was created to be the _____.

   • Woman was created to be the _____.

   • Man was created to exercise loving _____ over woman.

   • Woman was created to extend glad _____ to man.

3. God created men and women as a reflection of the _____.

   • The Persons of the Trinity are equally _____.

   • The Persons of the Trinity are positionally _____.

   • This is loving authority and glad submission in the context of beautiful _____.

THREE CONCLUSIONS ABOUT MANHOOD AND WOMANHOOD

1. All this is _____ for us.

   • Unity in diversity: we are attracted to each other by our _____.

   • Equality amid intimacy: we honor each other as we _____ each other.

2. All this is _____ to God.

   • We reflect God's _____.

   • We trust God's _____.

3. All this is the essence of the _____.

   • Christ is our _____ groom.

   • We are Christ's _____ bride.

   • God has designed the headship of men and the help of women to display the _____ of Christ to the culture around us.

Video sessions available for purchase at www.lifeway.com/counterculture

DISCUSS THE DVD SEGMENT WITH YOUR GROUP, USING THE QUESTIONS BELOW.

What was most helpful, encouraging, or challenging in this session? Why?

Provide examples showing that sexuality is one of the most sensitive issues in our culture today. How are issues of sexuality, gender, and marriage under attack, not only in culture but also within the church today?

How is the focus of this week's study also related to the image of God?

What biblical evidence shows that men and women are created with equal dignity but distinct and different roles?

How do Jesus and the Trinity help us see a biblical picture of authority, submission, equality, and distinction?

Why does our culture resist the idea of authority and submission as bad?

In what areas of life are you tempted to say, "I'm going to obey what the Bible says instead of truly believing that God's design is good"? What's the difference?

How is marriage a picture of the gospel and our relationship with God in Christ?

How does the gospel compel action related to issues of sexuality?

How do issues of sexuality open a door to conversations about the gospel? Give examples of statements that relate the gospel to sexuality, gender, and marriage.

THIS WEEK

Memorize Genesis 2:24 and pray for conviction and compassion as God opens your eyes to His good, pleasing, and perfect will for gender, sexuality, and marriage. Confess and repent of any sexual sin in your life, past or present, and commit to glorifying God with your body.

READ week 4 and complete the activities before the next group experience.
READ chapters 6–7 in the book *Counter Culture* by David Platt (Tyndale, 2015).

SEXUALITY

> *A man shall leave his father and his mother and hold fast to his wife, and they shall become one flesh.*
> Genesis 2:24

"*Evangelicalism is deeply infiltrated with the world spirit of our age when it comes to marriage and sexual morality. … There are those who call themselves evangelicals and who are among evangelical leadership who completely deny the biblical pattern for male and female relationships in the home and church. There are many who accept the idea of equality without distinction and deliberately set aside what the Scriptures teach at this point.*"[1]
Francis Schaeffer

"*The stakes in the current conflict over sex are more critical, more central, and more essential than in any controversy the church has ever known. This is a momentous statement, but I make it soberly, without exaggeration. Conflict over sex these days is not just challenging tradition, orthodoxy, and respect for authority in areas such as ordination, marriage, and gender roles. And it does not just affect critically important doctrines like the sanctity of human life, the authority and trustworthiness of scripture, the Trinity, and the incarnation of Christ. Rather, war over sex among Christians is now raging over absolutely essential matters of faith without which no one can truly be a Christian in the first place—matters such as sin, salvation, the gospel, and the identity of God himself.*"[2]
Daniel R. Heimbach

Loving our neighbor and respecting the equal dignity of all people don't mean what our culture would have us believe. This week we'll see that men and women are created distinctly and intentionally. Gender, sexuality, and marriage are all part of God's beautiful design.

---

1. Francis Schaeffer, *The Complete Works of Francis A. Schaeffer* (Wheaton, IL: Crossway Books, 1982), 398.

2. Daniel R. Heimbach, *True Sexual Morality: Recovering Biblical Standards for a Culture in Crisis* (Wheaton, IL: Crossway Books, 2004), 33–34.

DAY 1
GOD & GENDER

According to our culture, sexual differences are merely social constructions. Gender is biological chance. Some would even say that it's a preference, even if biology determines otherwise. If a person says they're male, female, or neither, then who's to say otherwise? Shouldn't it be their choice?

Sure, men and women have physical distinctions, but even these can be changed if someone so chooses. Aside from this, men and women are equal—and by *equal* our culture means identical. People are people, right? There's no difference. If this is our line of thought, it makes total sense for people's gender to be as subjective as their fashion. If it's socially acceptable to change hairstyle, change clothing, or even surgically modify our physical appearance, then what's different about changing our gender? Why is it acceptable to change practically anything about our appearance except gender? And who's to say a person can have sexual relations with and marry only a person of the opposite gender? Why get hung up on traditional views of men and women? There's no difference since we're identical. We're beyond that now as a society. This is what our culture says.

What changes in cultural opinion have you noticed regarding gender?

What's masculine according to our culture? What makes an ideal man?

What's feminine according to our culture? What makes an ideal woman?

But what does God say? Once again, let's look back at the creation of human beings. The opening pages of human history provide foundational truths about men and women and our relationships with God and one another. The importance of these foundational truths can't be overemphasized. And though many people today feel that the Bible is antiquated in its views on gender, those same people may be shocked to realize that these verses in Genesis are actually quite radical, historically.

We read this passage last week, but today let's focus on something a little different.

Read Genesis 1:26-27.

Underline the words *us, our,* and *them.*

Circle the words *image, male,* and *female.*

What do these verses reveal about God's design for human gender?

There are various opinions about exactly why God used the plural pronouns *us* and *our* to refer to Himself in this unique act of creation. However, the Bible is absolutely clear about the fact that men and women are both created in the image of God and that we experience a unique relationship with God. So in that sense, yes, men and women are absolutely equal. They are noted as equally created in the image of God yet distinct as created to be male and female. Equal yet distinct.

Here we see a glimpse of the Trinity. The one true God is revealed as three Persons: Father, Son, and Holy Spirit. Equal yet distinct. God isn't an impersonal force, but in a beautifully mysterious way, He exists in perfect relationship within the Trinity. Three in one. God didn't need to create the world and humanity. He wasn't lacking anything. God was and is perfect, complete, and infinite. Yet in His goodness He chose to create everything, including men and women. "Let us make man in our image" (v. 26), God said about humankind.

Men and women made in His image could share in the joy of a personal relationship with God—Father, Son, and Holy Spirit. This ability and opportunity to relate to God were unique. Nothing else in all creation bore the image of God. Men and women alone were made in the likeness of God though not identical to Him. He was infinite; they were finite. He was divine; they were human. He was Spirit; they were flesh. Yet in a way that nothing else in all creation can, men and women shared certain moral, intellectual, and relational capacities with God. They had the power to reason, the desire to love, the ability to speak, and the capacity to make moral decisions. God created them, blessed them, and gave them authority over the rest of His creation (see Gen. 1:28).

Man and woman were God's image bearers. He commanded them to be fruitful, multiplying His image throughout His creation, filling the earth with the glory of the Creator.

But this command wasn't just a theological metaphor. It was literal and practical. God expected procreation. Multiplication would have been impossible if God had created humans male and male or female and female. God's unique design enabled them to carry out His command.

This divine design involved far more than the capacity to reproduce, as important as that was. There was something greater than mere genetics here. There was enjoyment. God created man and woman to cherish their shared equality while complementing their various differences. He designed man and woman for sexual intimacy. We'll look more at this later this week, but see that the blessing and command of God involved sexual intimacy and biological reproduction through physical differences. Mutual benefit and pleasure resulted from being equal yet distinct.

Read Genesis 2:18.

If you remember the pattern of creation from last week, what was God's repeated declaration?

For the first time in Scripture and in human history, God declared something "not good." What was it?

Why is it significant that sin hasn't yet entered the world when it wasn't good for man to be alone?

What's the word used by God to describe the woman He created? Why is this significant?

Read Genesis 2:22-23.

God didn't have to create the woman this way, but He did. Why is the manner in which God created the woman significant?

God decides to make "a helper" (v. 18)—a suitable partner fit for the man and for the work God had given to him. When man fell asleep, God performed the first surgery, taking a rib from man's side. When the man opened his eyes, he was stunned, to say the least. The first words a human being is ever recorded saying were poetry, as the man sang in awe of woman.

Don't miss the magnificence of this scene. God brought man to realize that he needed someone equal to him, made with the same nature that he possessed but different from him, in order to help him do things he could never do on his own. This is precisely what God gave to man in woman, and the stage was thus set for the institution of marriage, which we'll look at in greater detail later this week.

In what ways have you seen the cultural argument that *equal* means *identical?*

This is where any Bible-informed conversation about men and women must begin: with men and women both being created with equal dignity before God and each other. Men and women both share in the inexpressible worth of creatures formed in the image of God Himself. In this way God speaks loudly from the start of Scripture against any sort of male or female superiority or dominance in the world.

Near the end of Scripture, God refers to men and women as fellow "heirs … of the grace of life" (1 Pet. 3:7). According to God's design, men are never to be perceived as better than women, and women are never to be perceived as better than men. We've seen that God abhors any treatment of men or women as inferior objects to be used or abused. For all eternity no gender will be greater than the other. No one should feel superior or inferior by nature of being a man or a woman.

EQUAL YET DISTINCT. MEN AND WOMEN ARE BOTH CREATED

IN THE IMAGE OF GOD. BY DESIGN WE'RE NOT IDENTICAL.

DAY 2
FOUNDATIONAL BREAKDOWN

The first sin in the world occurred not as a reaction to a generic temptation but as a response to a gender-specific test. The serpent's design in deceiving the couple was a deliberate subversion of God's design in creating the couple in the first place.

Read Genesis 2:16-17.

Whom did God entrust with the responsibility of carrying out the divine command?

Immediately following this command, God declared that it wasn't good for man to be alone, and He decided to make a helper suitable for him, as we studied yesterday.

Read Genesis 3:1-6.

Whom does the serpent engage in discussion and, consequently, in temptation?

Why is this significant?

Notice verse 6. Where is the man?

Why is this significant?

Instead of taking responsibility for protecting himself and his wife from temptation, man silently sat by. Man wimped out, abdicating his position of loving leadership. In this original sin we see not only the failure of the first person but also the first denial of God's clear word and good authority in our lives in order to follow the behavior and opinion of others. This was the beginning of culture's rift with God's design. From the very first couple, there's been a need to counter the culture we're in.

Notice that woman didn't have to convince man. There was no overt peer pressure, manipulation, playing mind games, or working his emotions. It simply says she took the fruit, ate, and handed "some to her husband who was with her, and he ate" too (v. 6). Instead of leading, he followed her lead. Instead of helping, she hurt them both. They were created equal yet distinct. They failed equally yet distinctly. They sinned—together—against God.

Read Genesis 3:8-13.

Describe the man and woman's relationship with God following their sin.

Describe their relationship with each other following their sin.

Remember, the core of sin is to deny God's goodness and sufficiency, rebelling against His loving authority in our lives.

In what ways does our culture reject what you know God has clearly said?

What do we see in this passage about God's intent for His commands and any apparent limitations or restrictions He sets on what we should or shouldn't do?

When God confronted him in his sin, the man had the audacity to blame his wife. In all this the world witnesses the first spineless abdication of a man's responsibility to love, serve, protect, and care for his wife. But he didn't stop there. Notice that he not only blamed the woman but also indirectly blamed God: "It was that woman that You gave to me, God. So it's either her fault or Yours." He got two accusations in before admitting any part in the whole thing. The woman immediately chimed in that she wasn't to blame either. Now she was following the man's lead, but the example was one of passivity and victimization. Nobody was to blame, they said.

How do you see this same attitude of making excuses and abdicating responsibility in our culture?

Specifically related to men, how does our culture allow or encourage men to pass blame and say, "Not my fault"?

Specifically related to women, how does our culture allow or encourage women to pass blame and say, "Not my fault"?

Read Genesis 3:14-24.

What's the consequence for the man's sin (vv. 17-19)?

What's the consequence for the woman's sin (v. 16)?

How do you see both judgment and grace, holiness and love, in God's response?

Notice a glimpse of the gospel here. Verse 15 has been called the *protoevangelium,* meaning *first gospel.* Immediately, God came to His people, judged sin, and promised deliverance. Jesus, born of a woman, would be wounded but ultimately victorious over sin, death, and our Enemy.

Again, the grace extended by God wasn't merely prophetic but practical. He not only promised a future hope and deliverance for all who confess their sin and submit their lives to the loving authority of the Savior, but He also provided clothing in the moment to cover their shameful nakedness. Even the banishment from the garden was an act of both judgment and grace.

How have you experienced God's provision and grace in the midst of your sin?

SUBMISSION AND AUTHORITY

For men today, the pendulum can swing too far in either direction. On the one extreme, we see spineless abdication of his responsibility in society and in marriage. On the other extreme, we see a selfish abuse of authority in society or in his marriage. One effect of sin is the tendency for a man to overcompensate and rule his wife in a forceful and oppressive way that denigrates woman's equal dignity with him. This is a fundamental misunderstanding of what it means to be a man and a woman.

This misunderstanding is one of the primary reasons submission and authority are such unpopular and uncomfortable terms for us today—because we've seen the dangerous ways these ideas have been exploited. Particularly in marriage relationships, we think of men who mistreat their wives emotionally, verbally, and even physically in order to show they're in control, men who selfishly use their wives to get what they want when they want it, no matter how their wives feel or are affected.

The corresponding effects in women's lives are additionally clear. Women are equally susceptible to a sinful distortion of God's design for them. A wife is prone to do what she wants when she wants, regardless of what her husband says or does. *He's not in charge; I am,* she thinks, literally working against her husband and his role of leadership in marriage. As a result, she defies not only her husband but ultimately God.

Do you see how the work of Satan in Genesis 3 is a foundational attack not just on humanity in general but specifically on men, women, and marriage? Husbands waffle back and forth between abdicating their responsibility to love and abusing their authority to lead. Wives, in response, will distrust such love and defy such leadership.

Which extreme do you naturally gravitate toward?

Inferiority/Passivity   Superiority/Domination

In the middle are love and respect, trust and provision, submission and headship.

"We can say then that a relationship of authority and submission between equals, with mutual giving of honor, is the most fundamental and most glorious interpersonal relationship in the universe. Such a relationship allows there to be interpersonal differences without 'better' or 'worse,' without 'more important' and 'less important.' And when we begin to dislike the very idea of authority and submission—not distortions and abuses, but the very idea—we are tampering with something very deep. We are beginning to dislike God Himself."[1]
Wayne A. Grudem

Our culture resists authority. We feel that different roles necessarily mean different worth or dignity. We think submission and subordination to authority are inherently bad and degrading. Any hierarchy like that is oppressive, right? But that's not what the Son of God thinks. He's eternally subject to the Father. His submission to the Father's authority is good, noble, wonderful, loving, equal in worth but different in role (see 1 Cor. 11:3). Equal yet distinct.

Read Matthew 26:39.

Using Jesus' example, record a short prayer of loving submission and trust in God's will.

1. Wayne A. Grudem, *Evangelical Feminism & Biblical Truth: An Analysis of More than One Hundred Disputed Questions*
   (Wheaton, IL: Crossway, 2004), 48.

DAY 3
SEXUAL MORALITY

Regardless of how you rank the current controversy over sexual immorality, it's clear that the most fundamental questions about what it means to be a Christian and whether we should submit to God's Word are at stake in this issue.

Today we're going to look at three major moral categories—heterosexual marriage, singleness, and homosexual behavior—and introduce one foundational truth—a biblical view of the body.

YOUR BODY

God created us as sexual beings. We're men and women with bodies that have been made in God's image for God's glory.

Read 1 Corinthians 6:12-13.

Paul quoted and refuted the pop culture of his day.

What's meant by "All things are lawful for me" (twice in v. 12)?

How is this mentality still popular in our culture today?

What were Paul's three responses?

How does this wisdom relate to any potentially addictive or abusive desire or behavior?

Verse 13 is vital for understanding God's design for us. Our bodies have been created not only by God but also for God. This truth counters the cultural perspective of our day. We're consumed with whatever can bring our bodies the most pleasure. The same was true in Corinth. The culture in which Paul was writing this letter was the height (or depth) of indulgence. In fact, "Corinth became a synonym not only for wealth, luxury, drunkenness and debauchery, but also for filth."[1] Part of the Corinthian culture was frequenting the temple of Aphrodite, the goddess of love, and engaging with at least one of more than one thousand cult prostitutes. Although we may not have cult prostitutes, our culture certainly idolizes sex and personal indulgence.

But what if our bodies haven't ultimately been created for self-gratification? What if our bodies have actually been created for God-glorification? And even better, what if God-glorification is actually the way to experience the greatest satisfaction in our bodies?

Look back at that phrase in verse 13: the body is meant "for the Lord, and the Lord for the body." Not only are our bodies designed for God, but God is also devoted to our bodies. Literally, He's for our bodies. God wants us to experience the maximum joy for which our bodies are built, and as the Creator of our bodies, He knows what will bring them the most pleasure. This takes us back to one of the core truths of the gospel: the reality that God loves us and is for us. God desires the best for us, and He designed our bodies not just for His glory but also for our good.

Read 1 Corinthians 6:14-20.

What was Paul's rationale for abstaining from sexual sin (see vv. 14-16)?

What was Paul's practical advice about sexual immorality (see v. 17)?

What reasons did he give for fleeing sexual sin?

Verse 18:

Verse 19:

Verse 20:

Summarize the biblical perspective on your body presented in 1 Corinthians 6:12-20.

Ultimately, God prohibits sexual worship—the idolization of sex and infatuation with sexual activity as a fundamental means to personal fulfillment. Throughout Scripture and history, people have mistakenly fallen into the trap of thinking that the God-created pleasure of sex and sexuality will bring us ultimate satisfaction (see Prov. 7:1-27; 1 Cor. 10:8). Sadly, it seems that we're no different in our time. All across our culture, people believe, *If only I have sexual freedom in this way or that way, then I'll be happy*. But this isn't true. Sex is good, but sex isn't God. It won't ultimately fulfill. Like any other idol, it will always take more than it gives while diverting the human heart away from the only One who's able to give supreme joy. Whenever God gives us a negative command, He always gives two positives to us: He provides us with something better while also protecting us from something worse. These simple truths help us see more clearly what we're doing when we ignore God's design.

HETEROSEXUAL MARRIAGE

In His love for us, God has identified the best use of our bodies, and He's been specific about our sexuality. As we've seen from the very beginning of the Bible, God designed a man's and a woman's body to join together as "one flesh" in marriage (Gen. 2:24). The language of "one flesh" points to the personal nature of this union. Sex isn't a mechanical act between two objects; it's a relational bond between two people. And not just any two people. This physical union is designed by God for a man and a woman who've committed their lives in a covenant relationship with each other (see Prov. 5:3-20; Mal. 2:14). There isn't one instance in all of God's Word where God advocates or celebrates sex outside a marriage relationship between a husband and a wife. Not one.

Read 1 Corinthians 7:1-5.

What countercultural truth is presented here about sex in the marriage relationship?

Our bodies are for the Lord, first and foremost, as temples of His Spirit. Then we become one flesh as husband and wife, and our bodies belong to each other. Scripture testifies here to the unique pleasure of sexual intimacy and the intense desire for sexual intimacy. Contrary to popular misconception, Christians, God, and the Bible are all very pro-sex. God created it. He created us. He made sex more than functional. He made it enjoyable.

Unfortunately, this is an area in which the church in our culture has done a poor job and a tremendous disservice to Christians. Simply saying no and teaching that sex is bad until you get married and then suddenly expecting a husband and wife to flip a switch now that they're allowed to engage in and enjoy a sexual relationship is naïve, at best. It's emotionally, relationally, and even spiritually damaging at times.

If you find that hard to believe or have trouble shifting gears mentally and emotionally after years of feeling guilt and shame for sexual activity, even for enjoying your spouse within the covenant of marriage, read Song of Solomon. An entire book of the Bible is devoted to romantic love, physical attraction, and sexual desire.

What were you taught about sex when you were young?

Did it have a positive, negative, or neutral effect on your behavior, your attitude toward sex, and your view of others?

How would you express both the beauty of sexual activity within marriage as well as the harm of sexual activity outside God's design?

God's good design for sex is the reason Scripture uses such strong language in prohibiting sexual activity outside marriage. The Bible calls this adultery, and it's forbidden in the Ten Commandments (see Ex. 20:14; also see Lev. 20:10; Prov. 6:28-32). But this isn't just an Old Testament command. Jesus and New Testament writers reiterated this restriction (see Matt. 19:7-9; Rom. 13:9; Heb. 13:4). According to God, sex with anyone who isn't your husband or your wife is sin, whether that happens before marriage, during marriage, or after marriage.

Not only is it contrary to God's design and therefore wrong to meditate on or act on sexual desire for others outside marriage, but it's also wrong to provoke sexual desires in others outside of marriage. God forbids immodest clothing (see 1 Tim. 2:9-10) and sternly warns against seductive speech (see Prov. 4:23; 5:1-23; 7:1-27). In addition, God prohibits any kind of crude speech, humor, or entertainment that remotely revolves around sexual immorality (see Eph. 5:3-5). Addressing the sex-crazed culture surrounding the church in the first century, God said, "It is shameful even to speak of the things that they do in secret" (Eph. 5:12).

In what seemingly harmless behavior (according to our culture) did God's Word bring conviction as you read the previous paragraph, and what will you do in response?

SINGLENESS

If you're single, don't engage in sexual activity. Not just for your own good but for the sake of the gospel. It's the ultimate in hypocrisy today to see young, single evangelicals, who are often incredibly passionate about social issues like poverty and slavery, simultaneously undercutting the social fabric of marriage through sex outside marriage. According to one "nationally representative study of young adults, just under 80 percent of unmarried, church-going, conservative Protestants who are currently dating someone are having sex of some sort."[2]

Scripture clearly speaks to single men and women. For those who have a strong sexual desire for marriage, God's Word exhorts single men and women to be married (see 1 Cor. 7:2). The onus here is particularly on men, whom God designed to take the initiative in the marriage relationship. Without question, this call to pursue a wife goes against the grain of current cultural trends that minimize the importance of marriage.

At the same time, Scripture also contains exhortations to singles who are waiting for a husband or a wife, as well as men and women whom God specifically calls to singleness. The apostle Paul put himself in the latter category, even saying, "I wish that all were as I myself am … in view of the present distress" (1 Cor. 7:7,26). In view of the persecution and perversion that surrounded Paul in first-century culture, he advocated remaining single in favor of "undivided devotion to the Lord" (1 Cor. 7:35). Scripture thus encourages all single men and women, as long as they're single, to maximize their singleness through a commitment to Christ and His commission in the culture around us.

Read 1 Corinthians 7:32-35.

What unique spiritual opportunity exists for a single man or woman?

HOMOSEXUAL BEHAVIOR

The design of marriage in Genesis 2 is sufficient to establish God's prescribed pattern for sexual union between a man and a woman. But the Bible is clear and consistent, affirming from cover to cover that homosexual activity is sexual immorality before God. Yet just like Adam and Eve, we're tempted not just in our culture but in the church to subject God's Word to our judgment.

If someone wants to advocate for homosexual activity, he or she must maintain that the Bible is irrelevant to modern humanity, inconsistent with our experience, and thus insufficient as a source of truth and guidance for our lives. The reality is that as soon as we advocate homosexual activity, we undercut biblical authority. And in the process of undercutting the authority of the Bible, we undermine the integrity of the entire gospel. For if the Bible is wrong about certain issues, then what else is the Bible wrong about?

Read 1 Corinthians 6:9-10.

Why is it significant that Paul instructed the Christians in Corinth not to be deceived?

How is the American church at risk of being deceived?

Read Romans 1:22-32.

What do people mean when they say, "I'm born this way"?

We're all born sinners. Every one of our hearts is predisposed to sin. But that doesn't excuse or justify our tendency toward any particular sin. The opposite is true. We're confessing our need for a Savior to redeem us and transform our desires because we all inherit hearts bent toward sin.

Ever since Adam and Eve sinned in the garden, every person born of a man and a woman has inherited this sinful heart. We may all have different biological heritages, but we all share one common spiritual inheritance: sin. And we all share one common need: salvation (see Rom. 5:12-21).

1. William Barclay, *The Letters to the Corinthians* (Louisville, KY: Westminster John Knox Press, 2002), 3.
2. Mark Regnerus, "The Case for Early Marriage," *Christianity Today* [online], 31 July 2009 [cited 28 November 2014].
   Available from the Internet: *christianitytoday.com*.

MARRIAGE

Marriage is arguably the most prominent issue in our culture today and will likely prove to be the most polarizing and divisive, possibly becoming the decisive issue for the direction and position of the church in this generation. It's the sum total of the other issues we've studied this week: gender and sexuality.

Is the discussion of marriage in our culture simply a matter of moving on from old-fashioned and traditional ways of thinking to progressive and open-minded ways of thinking? Is marriage merely a tradition that's open to changing with the times? If so, it stands to reason that it needs to be updated. If merely a tradition, there may be sentiment tied up in it, but really there's no harm to our culture or even to our churches if it changes. Or is marriage an institution that was ordained to be consistent through all time? Is it representative of something deeper, something spiritual? Is it hateful to recognize the gospel as not only applicable but also foundational to marriage?

How does our culture define *marriage*?

This question lies at the heart of what amounts to a moral revolution in the time and culture in which we live. For millennia civilizations have defined *marriage* as an exclusive, permanent union of a man and a woman with each other. Merely two decades ago, politicians in our country voted across party lines to defend this definition of marriage in what was called the Defense of Marriage Act. Yet in June 2013 the Supreme Court of the United States struck down the Defense of Marriage Act, paving the way for the complete redefinition of marriage across our culture. In the days that followed, states began officially defining marriage according to different terms, now notably identifying same-sex relationships as so-called marriages.

In reality, however, the court's decision in 2013 represents only one part of a much larger trend away from traditional marriage across our culture that's taken place over many years. Though it's difficult to obtain precise data, census figures show that nearly half of all first marriages today end in divorce (a number that only increases with second and third marriages). That's if men and women even decide to marry. The number of cohabiting couples in our culture has nearly quadrupled over the past 30 years as more and more singles postpone or put aside marriage altogether. Marital union is clearly on the decline. In the past 40 years the number of independent female households in our culture increased by 65 percent, and the number of independent male households leapt by 120 percent.[1] Less than half of all homes in America today are inhabited by married couples.[2]

Marriage is under attack. But it's too important to surrender. It's not hateful to boldly defend what God has ordained.

Read Ephesians 5:22-24.

Why are these verses offensive in our culture?

In 1 Corinthians 11:3 Paul wrote, "The head of a wife is her husband, and the head of Christ is God." Paul was teaching that there are headship and submission in God Himself. So is that bad? Is that chauvinistic of the Father? Is that offensive to the Son? Not at all. It's good.

Even right now the Son is sitting at the Father's right hand (see Rom. 8:34; Heb. 1:3; 1 Pet. 3:22). Never does the Father sit at the Son's right hand. So the Son never says to the Father, "This isn't fair to Me. Why do You get to be in charge simply because You're the Father? The Son never says to the Father, This is not good. You've been in charge the past 50 billion years now. Why don't You let Me be in charge for the next 50 billion? No, this is good. And if it's good for God, why wouldn't it be good for us too? Who are we to think we have a better way?

According to God's design, what's the woman's role in marriage?

Why is it significant that verse 22 says wives should "submit to your own husbands"?

How is the woman's response to her own husband an act of worship and a picture of the church's relationship to Christ?

Read Ephesians 5:25-33.

According to God's design, what's the man's role in marriage?

What does it mean for Christ to be the Head of the church?

In these eight verses how many times is the husband commanded to love his wife?

This passage makes it clear that a husband is to love his wife unselfishly. The world tells men to defend themselves, assert themselves, and draw attention to themselves, yet the Word tells men to sacrifice themselves for their wives. Headship isn't an opportunity to control wives; it's a responsibility to die for them.

This means, husband, you don't love your wife because of what you get from her. That's how the culture defines *love*. That's selfish. Godly love is sacrificial. The culture says you love your wife because of her attractive attributes and compelling characteristics, but this is a wildly fickle preference that we're calling love. For as soon as some attribute or characteristic fades, then love fails. Husbands, love your wives not because of who they are but because of who Christ is. He loves them deeply, and your responsibility is to reflect His love.

Obviously, husbands don't do all Christ has done; namely, they don't die for the sins of their wives. Yet they live for the sanctification of their wives. Husbands live to serve their wives and to see them grow in Christlikeness. Men are accountable for loving their wives in such a way that they grow in loveliness. Just as Christ takes responsibility for the spiritual health of His church, men are responsible for the spiritual health of their wives and their marriages. A man is to treasure, encourage, build up, and comfort his wife. A man takes the initiative in caring for his wife, not waiting for her to approach him with problems that need to be fixed.

If you're a husband, ask your wife the following question regularly and sincerely (if you're not married, remember this): "How can I love you and lead our marriage better?"

Couples, realize what's at stake here: you're representing Christ and His church to a watching world in the way you treat each other.

If you're married, what would the relationship with your spouse communicate to the world about Christ and the church?

What does it reveal to you? In what specific way are you convicted by God's Word?

Read Ephesians 5:33.

What's the husband commanded to do?

What's the wife commanded to do?

Based on what we've studied so far this week, what can you conclude from the fact that the commands aren't identical?

Obviously, that doesn't mean love and respect shouldn't both be expressed by each spouse, but God's Word is subtly yet clearly pointing out that God has created women with a unique need to be loved and men with a unique need to be respected.

These needs are related to God's design of the man in a position of loving headship and the woman in a position of respectful helpmate. Practically speaking, a wife can more easily respect her husband if she feels loved. A wife who feels loved will more naturally submit to her husband's lead. After all, he's acting in love for her. Likewise, when the husband feels respected, he's more confident to lead his wife and to love her sacrificially. When his unique need is being met, his desire is to meet her unique need. There's a mutually beneficial and fulfilling enjoyment of each other. In giving and receiving, there's an equality. Neither his need nor hers is superior. Although the needs are distinct, both are equally worthy of being fulfilled.

If married, how can you express the love or respect your spouse needs?

How does remembering that these needs are part of God's design encourage and enable you to meet the unique needs of your spouse?

Women often find it easier to love their husbands than to respect them. A woman can sit with other women and speak about her husband disrespectfully but then quietly go home and care for his needs. Why? Because she loves him. But the more important question is, does she respect him? When a wife is trying to work on a troubled marriage, she may tell her husband that she loves him, which is what she would like to hear. But again, the more important question is, does she respect her husband, and does she tell him that she respects him?

A wife may think, *My husband doesn't work hard enough or do enough to earn my respect.* But even then, might such a wife be buying into the unbiblical lie that respect is purely based on performance? In the same way a selfless love for his wife is based on God's charge to him, isn't a wife's selfless respect for her husband based on God's charge to her?

So wives, you're in a complementary, not competitive, relationship with your husband. Yield to leadership in love, knowing you're representing the church's relationship with Christ.

Behold the beauty of God's design for man, woman, and marriage. Two dignified people, both molded in the image of their Maker. Two diverse people, uniquely designed to complement each other. A male and a female fashioned by God to form one flesh, a physical bond between two bodies where the deepest point of unity is found at the greatest point of difference. A matrimony marked by unity in diversity, equality with variety, and personal satisfaction through shared consummation.

PRAY THAT GOD WILL BE GLORIFIED

THROUGH CHRIST-CENTERED MARRIAGES.

1. Mark Regnerus, "The Case for Early Marriage," *Christianity Today* [online], 31 July 2009 [cited 1 December 2014]. Available from the Internet: *christianitytoday.com.*
2. "America's Families and Living Arrangements, 2012" [online], August 2013 [cited 1 December 2014]. Available from the Internet: *census.gov.*

A GOSPEL RESPONSE TO ISSUES OF GENDER & SEXUALITY

None of this was haphazard. From the beginning of time, God designed men, women, and marriage for a purpose. That purpose wasn't fully revealed until Jesus died on the cross, rose from the dead, and instituted the church.

After all this the Bible looks back to the institution of marriage and asserts, "This mystery [of marriage] is profound, and … it refers to Christ and the church" (Eph. 5:32). When God made man, then woman, and brought them together in a relationship called marriage, he wasn't simply rolling the dice, drawing some straws, or flipping a coin. He was painting a picture. His intent from the start was to illustrate His faithful and sacrificial love for people.

This is why biblical marriage is worth defending in the face of cultural redefinition, because God established marriage at the beginning of creation to be one of the primary means by which He broadcasts the gospel to a watching world. As husbands sacrifice their lives for the sake of their wives—loving, leading, serving, protecting, and providing for them—the world gets a glimpse of God's grace. Sinners see that Christ has gone to a cross where He suffered, bled, and died for them so that they could experience eternal salvation through submission to Him.

They also see in a wife's relationship with her husband that such submission isn't a burden to bear. Marriage onlookers observe a wife joyfully and continually experiencing her husband's sacrificial love for her and then gladly and spontaneously submitting in selfless love to him. In this visible representation of the gospel, the world realizes that following Christ isn't a matter of forced duty. Instead, it's a means to full, eternal, and absolute delight.

Read Proverbs 14:12.

Record Proverbs 14:12 in the space below.

How is our culture headed in a direction that seems right to it regarding gender, sexuality, and marriage?

Ultimately, all of God's plan is good for us and glorifying to Him. God has sent His Son to die for sinners, and He has set up marriage to reflect that reality. When we understand this, we realize that marriage exists even more for God than it does for us. God has designed marriage not only to satisfy our needs but also to display His glory in the gospel of Jesus Christ. When we realize this, we recognize that to declare the gospel to the world, we must defend marriage in the world. To defend marriage, we must recognize and honor the beautifully distinct and complementary roles of men and women. Gender is part of God's intentional design.

For these reasons it's altogether right to be grieved about the redefinition of marriage in our culture. So-called same-sex marriage is now recognized as a legitimate entity in the eyes of our government. Such a designation by a government, however, doesn't change a definition established by God. The only true marriage in the eyes of God remains the exclusive, permanent union of a man and a woman with each other, even as our Supreme Court and state legislatures deliberately defy this reality. Without question we're living in historically momentous days—days that are momentous in devastating ways.

Yet all most definitely isn't lost, for the opportunity for gospel witness is far greater today than it was even a couple of years ago. As spiritual darkness engulfs the biblical picture of marriage in our culture, spiritual light will stand out even more starkly in the portrait of a husband who lays down his life for his wife and a wife who joyfully follows her husband's loving leadership. Be sure of this: God's design for marriage is far more breathtaking and much more satisfying than anything we could ever create on our own. The more men and women manipulate marriage, the more we will discover that this kind of marriage or that kind of marriage won't fully gratify us, for only the Creator who designed marriage is able to finally and eternally satisfy us.

Read 1 Thessalonians 4:3-8.

What's God's will for (see v. 3) and call on (see v. 7) your life?

Notice again that what we do with our bodies has spiritual implications. When Paul elaborated on what he meant by sanctification—growing in holiness—it may be surprising that he didn't include what we typically consider spiritual disciplines. Rather, he noted a couple of practical matters in a Christ follower's personal relationships.

What specific things did Paul note as signs of growing spiritually in Christlikeness?

What's the conclusion about people who are consumed with their lusts and disregard this teaching?

How does the gospel shape what you believe about identity and gender roles? Record a simple statement of what you believe.

How do conversations about gender open opportunities to share the gospel? Record a simple statement explaining how this particular issue is rooted in a foundational understanding of the gospel and our relationship with God.

How does the gospel shape what you believe about sexual morality? Record a simple statement of what you believe.

How do conversations about sexual morality open opportunities to share the gospel? Record a simple statement explaining how this particular issue is rooted in a foundational understanding of the gospel and our relationship with God.

How does the gospel shape what you believe about marriage? Record a simple statement of what you believe.

How do conversations about marriage open opportunities to share the gospel? Record a simple statement explaining how this particular issue is rooted in a foundational understanding of the gospel and our relationship with God.

Identify a specific time when you've been in a conversation or incident related to issues of gender, sexuality, or marriage. Describe the conversation and your perceived outcome.

Following this study, would you say or do anything differently?   YES   NO
How will you approach this issue in the future?

WEEK 5
RACE

WELCOME TO THIS FIFTH GROUP DISCUSSION OF *COUNTER CULTURE*.

What was most helpful, encouraging, or challenging in your study of week 4?

What issues of race have you seen in the news lately? Share a recent news story related to racism or immigration.

To prepare to view the DVD segment, read aloud Revelation 7:9-10.

After this I looked, and behold, a great multitude that no one could number, from every nation, from all tribes and peoples and languages, standing before the throne and before the Lamb, clothed in white robes, with palm branches in their hands, and crying out with a loud voice, "Salvation belongs to our God who sits on the throne, and to the Lamb!"
Revelation 7:9-10

COMPLETE THE VIEWER GUIDE BELOW AS YOU WATCH DVD SESSION 5.

From the very beginning, the story line of the Bible depicts a basic _____ behind worldly diversity.

Fundamentally, we're all part of the same _____.

A PICTURE OF UNITY AND DIVERSITY

1. See the _____ God has made.

   • From the very beginning of the Bible, God is promising to bring His blessing not just to one people but to _____ the peoples of the earth.

   • We work for ethnic harmony because of God's purpose in all of _____.

   • God is most glorified when His people are most _____.

2. See the _____ Christ has paid.

   • All of us who are a part of the human race are _____.

   • We all need a _____.

   • Christ shed His blood for every _____.

     Over _____ people groups are still unreached.

   • Christ shed His blood for every _____.

     Over _____ languages still have no Bible.

3. See the _____ God has prepared.

   • In the future we will _____ together in perfect harmony.

   • In the present we now _____ together for unity in our diversity.

Video sessions available for purchase at *www.lifeway.com/counterculture*

DISCUSS THE DVD SEGMENT WITH YOUR GROUP, USING THE QUESTIONS BELOW.

What was most helpful, encouraging, or challenging in this session? Why?

How does the issue of race relate to what we've already studied about gender?

How has the issue of race been wrongly defined?

How do Genesis 10 and Revelation 7 reshape our view of the issue of race?

How is defining someone by the color of their skin not only unhelpful but also eventually impossible?

How do we show a tendency, even with the gospel and our churches, to believe that we should focus on people like us?

How would you explain the need we all share regardless of ethnicity?

How does the gospel compel action related to issues of race?

How do issues of race open a door to conversations about the gospel? Give examples of statements that relates the gospel to issues of racism and immigration.

THIS WEEK

Memorize Revelation 7:9-10 and pray for God to help you see all people as being created in His image. Begin looking for ways to intentionally build relationships with people who aren't from the same ethnic background as you. Identify ways your church can reach out to and include more people of various backgrounds.

READ week 5 and complete the activities before the next group experience.
READ chapter 8 in the book *Counter Culture* by David Platt (Tyndale, 2015).

RACE

> *After this I looked, and behold, a great multitude that no one could number, from every nation, from all tribes and peoples and languages, standing before the throne and before the Lamb, clothed in white robes, with palm branches in their hands, and crying out with a loud voice, "Salvation belongs to our God who sits on the throne, and to the Lamb!"*
> Revelation 7:9-10

"I have a dream ... even though we face the difficulties of today and tomorrow, I still have a dream. ... I have a dream that one day this nation will rise up, live out the true meaning of its creed: 'We hold these truths to be self-evident, that all men are created equal.' ... I have a dream that my four little children will one day live in a nation where they will not be judged by the color of their skin but by the content of their character. ... I have a dream that one day every valley shall be exalted, and every hill and mountain shall be made low. The rough places will be made plain, and the crooked places will be made straight. And the glory of the Lord shall be revealed, and all flesh shall see it together."[1]
Martin Luther King Jr.

This week our study of the beauty in being created equal yet distinct broadens to issues of ethnicity. How does the church respond to issues of racism, immigration, and cultural diversity?

1. Martin Luther King Jr., "I Have a Dream ..." Speech at the March on Washington, 1963 [online, cited 1 December 2014]. Available from the Internet: *www.archives.gov/press/exhibits/dream-speech.pdf.*

DAY 1
ALL NATIONS

It all started with one family—a man and a woman created in the image of God—husband and wife joined together as one flesh and blessed by God.

From that point during the course of this study we've traced the story line through the creation of man (see Gen. 1–2), the fall of man (see Gen. 3), the downward spiral of sin (see Gen. 4–5), the grace of God and establishment of a covenant (see Gen. 6), the judgment of sin through flooding the world, and a picture of salvation for those who put their faith in God (see Gen. 7–8).

Read Genesis 9:1.

Along with God's blessing comes what command, echoed from the opening pages of Scripture with the creation of the first man and woman?

Read Genesis 10:32.

What does this verse say about every nation on the planet?

People began dividing according to their clans, their languages, their lands, and their nations. All those divisions traced their human ancestry back to one family, Noah and his sons (see Gen. 10). And then that ancestry traces back to one couple, Adam and Eve (see Gen. 5). This has been God's plan all along. Think back to our study of Acts 17 in week 1. This divine plan is precisely what Paul referenced in the New Testament when he told a crowd of philosophers in Athens:

> *[God] made from one man every nation of mankind to live on all the face of the earth, having determined allotted periods and the boundaries of their dwelling place.*
> Acts 17:26

The story line of Scripture depicts a basic unity behind worldly diversity. A common thread runs throughout the generations. From the beginning God designed a human family that would originate from one father and one mother.

Read Genesis 11:1-9.

How does the description in verses 2-4 reveal disobedience to the blessing and command given to Adam and to Noah?

God was determined to fill the earth He created with the people He created in His image and for His glory. In this story people chose to settle in one place, establish a name for themselves, and reach heaven through their own efforts. Once again, we see both judgment and grace.

Knowing God's desire for humankind, how was confusing the language both God's judgment and His grace?

What specific examples do you still see in our culture of the belief that humans can do anything to which we set our minds?

What encouragement or hope do you find in recognizing that God's faithfulness isn't derailed by man's sinfulness?

Men and women created in the image of God were finally beginning to spread out, multiplying and filling the earth. Different languages resulted in divisions among people groups. People naturally gravitated toward those most like themselves and distanced themselves from those seen as different. An us-versus-them mentality quickly saturated human hearts. Wickedness spilled over into wars among nations and conflicts among clans. The pages of human history are littered with an evil affinity for ethnic animosity.

These same pages reveal a God with a passion for all people groups. After the nations rebelled against Him at Babel in Genesis 11, God called a specific group of people to become His own in Genesis 12. That nation would descend from Noah, through Shem and Abram (see Gen. 11:10-32). God promised to bless these ethnic descendants of Abram, but the purpose of His blessing extended far beyond them.

Read Genesis 12:1-3.

What's God's promise? How was God's blessing more than just personal favor in Abram's life and family?

This promise is reiterated over and over in the Old Testament as God declared His desire for all nations to behold His greatness and experience His grace (see Ps. 96). In other words, God was doing what He was doing among His people, not just for His people's sake but for the sake of His name among all nations. And we see this emphasis throughout the Old Testament, from the very beginning through Psalms and the Prophets. Understanding this foundational desire enables us to read human history through a different lens. We can clearly see God at work to bring about His plan of blessing all nations. We recognize His love for unity and diversity. Difficult circumstances that may cause individuals to question God's goodness are better understood as part of a much bigger picture.

Think about what God was doing in the Book of Daniel, for example. Many of us know the story of Shadrach, Meshach, and Abednego being thrown into a fiery furnace because they wouldn't bow down and worship the king. Why would God let these three Hebrew servants who were loyal to Him be thrown into a fiery furnace? When we read that struggle, we miss the point if we don't get to Daniel 3:28-29. There we read that, as a result of their being thrown into that furnace and coming out on the other side without a drop of sweat on their brows, the king declared the God of Shadrach, Meshach, and Abednego was able to save His people and was worthy of glory among all the nations. That's a pagan king saying God deserves glory among all the nations.

It's the same thing in Daniel 6 when Daniel was thrown into a lion's den for having a quiet time. That'll make you think twice about having a quiet time in the morning if you know this is what happens. But Daniel did it anyway. He prayed. He opened the windows and prayed. And Daniel was thrown into a lion's den. Why? So that the next morning when he walked out alive and some other guys were thrown in, again a pagan king would declare that the God of Daniel was able to save His people and was worthy of glory among all peoples.

We have a tendency to think God's blessing is just for us or for people like us. In a sense we individually think God's promises and purposes center on us, but it's not true. The promise God has made is clear. All history is headed toward the day when worshipers from every tribe, tongue, and language will assemble around the throne of God and give Him the praise He's due. So that goal is anticipated from cover to cover in Scripture.

How would you explain God's desire for all people?

ETHNICITY

This leads us right to where the Bible grounds our understanding of human diversity: in human ethnicity. To use the language of Genesis 10, we compose "clans" in separate "nations" that speak different "languages" in diverse "lands." And with the globalization of the world and the migration of men and women across continents and into cities, these clans from separate nations and with different languages now often live in the same land.

Here the concept of ethnicity is immensely helpful, for it includes all these factors and more. Instead of being strictly tied to biology, ethnicity is much more fluid, factoring in social, cultural, lingual, historical, and even religious characteristics. While we commonly recognize approximately 200 nations in the world today, anthropological scholars have identified thousands (some say more than 11,000; others say more than 16,000) of distinct ethnolinguistic groups in the world. These groups, often called people groups, possess a common self-identity with common history, customs, patterns, and practices based on the two primary characteristics of ethnicity and language.

How does this understanding of human diversity and unity change the way you see people?

How does it change the way you understand Scripture and God's work in history?

DAY 2
IN THE CHURCH

The church is the community of God's people called out from every tribe, tongue, and nation.

In the New Testament we begin seeing the fulfillment of the promises God made in the Old Testament. Twenty-eight generations later, the Savior through whom every family on earth would be blessed was born to a young Jewish couple—descendants of Abraham (see Matt. 1:1-17). Jesus Christ lived in perfect trust and submission to the authority of God, without any sin. Jesus— God with us, the seed of a woman—lived, died, and was raised in victory over sin and death. Christ's death paid the penalty for man's sin, the ultimate act of God's judgment and grace.

Forty days following His resurrection, Jesus gathered His disciples for final instructions before returning to His Father's side.

Read Acts 1:1-11.

Underline the word *began* in verse 1. Why is it significant that verse 1 describes Jesus' earthly ministry as the beginning of His teaching and activity?

In what ways do you see Jesus disciples' attention redirected from a limited earthly perspective to spiritual priorities?

What did Jesus twice promise to give the disciples?

What mission did Jesus give His disciples? How does this mission relate to what you've been studying, especially the blessing and command God has been giving His people since Adam, Noah, and Abram?

Notice the disciples were still focused on themselves and on a desire for God to bless their ethnic group—the nation of Israel. Their mentality was still one of blessing through political, economic, and military power. But God had greater plans for a different kind of kingdom and influence.

> In what way are you personally obeying Jesus' command to be His witness on earth?

> Does your church focus on themselves and people most like them ethnically? Does your small group?

> How does your church reflect God's heart for all nations—all ethnic groups?

In our own short history our country and our churches haven't always reflected God's heart for seeing all people with equal dignity. Pastors and church members in the pre–Civil War United States who used God's Word to justify the practice of slavery were living in sin. The Bible clearly considers anything that undercuts the dignity of any man or woman as rebellion against God's character, a violation of God's Word, and a denial of God's gospel. Today slavery among 27 million people in the world represents similar rebellion against God's character, for contemporary slavery undercuts the truth in God's gospel that all men and women are created equal.

Read the sobering words of Martin Luther King Jr.:

> *"In the midst of blatant injustices inflicted upon the Negro, I have watched white churches stand on the sideline and merely mouth pious irrelevancies and sanctimonious trivialities. In the midst of a mighty struggle to rid our nation of racial and economic injustice, I have heard so many ministers say, 'Those are social issues with which the gospel has no real concern.'"*[1]

Then he pleaded for them to apply the gospel to such social issues, saying:

> *"There was a time when the church was very powerful. It was during that period when the early Christians rejoiced when they were deemed worthy to suffer for what they believed. In those days the church was not merely a thermometer that recorded the ideas and principles of*

popular opinion; it was a thermostat that transformed the mores of society. … But the judgment of God is upon the church as never before. If the church of today does not recapture the sacrificial spirit of the early church, it will lose its authentic ring, forfeit the loyalty of millions, and be dismissed as an irrelevant social club with no meaning for the twentieth century."[2]

Has our culture "dismissed [the church] as an irrelevant social club with no meaning" in the 21st century? In what ways would this be an accurate dismissal of many churches in our culture? In what ways does the church have more to offer than a homogenous social club?

Read Acts 2:1-11.

How was the miracle at Pentecost reversing what God did at the tower of Babel (see Gen. 11:1-9)?

Read Acts 2:36-41.

What must anyone do to be saved "from this crooked generation" (v. 40) and added to the church?

UNITY IN DIVERSITY

Remember what Jesus prayed before He went to the cross?

> *I do not ask for these only, but also for those who will believe in me through their word, that they may all be one, just as you, Father, are in me, and I in you, that they also may be in us, so that the world may believe that you have sent me. The glory that you have given me I have given to them, that they may be one even as we are one, I in them and you in me, that they may become perfectly one, so that the world may know that you sent me and loved them even as you loved me.*
> John 17:20-23

Look at that language. The people of God, the church composed of all peoples, will be one—perfectly united—so that the world can believe in the triune God. God is clearly most glorified when His people are most unified among diversity.

How can the world know Christ through the unity of the church?

What will you do to promote unity in your church? To whom do you need to reach out? To whom do you need to make amends?

The unity and diversity of the church are God's beautiful design. We share a bond stronger than any earthly family, greater than genetics. By the blood of our Savior, we have new life through faith in Him. The entire human race shares one Heavenly Father.

Read Galatians 3:28.

What has God taught you through someone of a different gender, culture, or ethnicity?

GOD IS GLORIFIED WHEN HIS PEOPLE ARE UNIFIED.

1. Martin Luther King Jr., *A Testament of Hope: The Essential Writings and Speeches of Martin Luther King Jr.* (New York: HarperCollins, 1991), 299.

2. Ibid., 300.

DAY 3
HEAVEN

Our culture has plenty of opinions—and jokes—when it comes to heaven. A Starbucks cup recently had this to say about the afterlife:

> "Heaven is totally overrated. It seems boring. Clouds, listening to people play the harp. It should be somewhere you can't wait to go, like a luxury hotel. Maybe blue skies and soft music were enough to keep people in line in the seventeenth century, but heaven has to step it up a bit. They're basically getting by because they only have to be better than hell."[1]

What idea have you heard about heaven?

On a scale of 1 to 10 (1 = indifferent, 10 = obsessed), how would you rate our culture's interest in heaven? Explain your answer.

1   10
|———|
Indifferent   Obsessed

Here's some good news. Heaven won't involve sitting back and listening to a harp on a cloud. Heaven will be the eternal enjoyment of the presence of God where we'll stand, where we'll sing, where we'll serve, and where we'll be satisfied in Him in a way no luxury hotel could ever compare. And we'll experience it together.

Read Revelation 5:9-10.

What does it mean to ransom?

Whom did Jesus—the Lamb of God—ransom?

With what did He purchase the freedom of His people?

Read Revelation 7:9-10.

What do these two pictures (Rev. 5:9-10; 7:9-10) reveal about people of different ethnicities?

See the glorious picture of what's to come. We began studying this last week, but it comes to the forefront here in Revelation 7. Every people and tribe is represented around the throne here. This scene isn't wishful thinking or happy thoughts on fluffy clouds. It's a rock-solid promise in the Word of God that all peoples will be represented in heaven, celebrating salvation in Christ.

In the world today anthropologists and ethnographers estimate that there are more than 11,000 different people groups who share distinct language and cultural characteristics. And Scripture teaches that every single one of them is going to be represented around the throne on this day.

This picture is the culmination of everything we've seen since the beginning of Scripture. If the establishment of the church and miracle of Pentecost were a reversal of Babel, then in Revelation we see the reversal of what happened in Genesis (and better). Again we see the tree of life but now with people having unlimited access to its fruit. From Genesis to Revelation we've gone from a single man and woman breaking fellowship with God and receiving the consequence of death to people of all nations inheriting eternal life:

> *The angel showed me the river of the water of life, bright as crystal, flowing from the throne of God and of the Lamb through the middle of the street of the city; also, on either side of the river, the tree of life with its twelve kinds of fruit, yielding its fruit each month. The leaves of the tree were for the healing of the nations.*
> Revelation 22:1-2

Read Revelation 21:1-8.

What does this Scripture reveal about each topic in this Bible study?

Countering culture:

Greed/idolatry:

Human life:

Sexual morality/marriage:

Race/Ethnicity:

Faith:

How does this biblical picture of eternal life give you hope and encouragement in the midst of difficult personal and cultural circumstances today?

All of human history is headed toward this end. Ultimately, the story has already been written. We know how it ends and where we are headed. Our Creator, the triune God, is our Savior. We are His bride. This earthly shadow will one day give way to its eternal substance. On that day Christ will be completely united with His church, and all of heaven will shout:

> *"Hallelujah! For the Lord our God the Almighty reigns. Let us rejoice and exult and give him the glory, for the marriage of the Lamb has come, and his Bride has made herself ready; it was granted her to clothe herself with fine linen, bright and pure"—for the fine linen is the righteous deeds of the saints. And the angel said to me, "Write this: Blessed are those who are invited to the marriage supper of the Lamb." And he said to me, "These are the true words of God."*
> Revelation 19:6-9

Unfortunately, Christian history is filled with a lack of understanding of how the gospel affects the way we view and love people of different ethnicities. The hope and prayer for you in this study is that this wouldn't be what the next generation will say about the church of our day. The body of Christ is a multicultural citizenry of an otherworldly kingdom, and this reality changes the way we live in this ever-evolving country. By the sheer grace of God in the gospel, we're compelled to resist ethnic pride and prejudice and to reflect gospel truth and grace as we look forward to the day when "a great multitude that no one [can] number, from every nation, from all tribes and peoples and languages" (Rev. 7:9) will stand as one redeemed race to give glory to the all-sovereign King who ransomed us by His blood.

How does Scripture shape the way Christians view people of various ethnicities?

Toward what person or group of people should your attitude change as a result of this biblical reality?

THIS WORLD ISN'T YOUR HOME. THE HEAVENLY FATHER IS PREPARING

A PLACE FOR CHILDREN OF EVERY TRIBE, TONGUE, AND NATION.

1. As quoted by Donald J. Johnson, *How to Talk to a Skeptic: An Easy-to-Follow Guide for Natural Conversations and Effective Apologetics* (Bloomington, MN: Bethany House Publishers, 2013), 118.

DAY 4
RACISM & IMMIGRATION

Imagine a scene where you walk into a room by yourself. There you see two tables, one with a group of people ethnically like you and the other with people ethnically unlike you. Instinctively, you gravitate toward one of these groups. We all do.

Which group do you naturally gravitate toward?

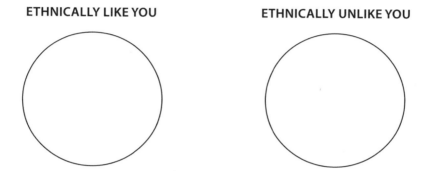

ETHNICALLY LIKE YOU

ETHNICALLY UNLIKE YOU

Why do you naturally gravitate toward certain people?

What does our culture say about diversity?

Consider the natural diversity (or lack thereof) in your social circles. How ethnically diverse are the places you …

WORK	LIVE	PLAY	WORSHIP

RACISM

Unless we're intentional about seeking more diverse relationships, our social circles will most often be fairly homogenous. Something in us assumes that those who are like us are safer, more comfortable, and therefore better for us. Similarly, we're prone to act as if those who are unlike us are less safe, less comfortable, and less beneficial. It seems, then, not to be a huge leap from such simple preference to the kind of sinful prejudice that stains the record of human— and church—history.

Since the time of the Civil Rights Movement, some have advocated for a colorblind society that pretends our differences don't exist. This, however, isn't what the gospel compels. The gospel doesn't deny the obvious ethnic, cultural, and historical differences that distinguish us from one another. Nor does the gospel suppose that these differences are merely superficial.

Instead, the gospel begins with a God who creates all men and women in His image, a God who then diversifies humanity according to clans and lands as a creative reflection of His grace and glory in distinct groups of people. Therefore, the gospel compels us to celebrate our ethnic distinctions, value our cultural differences, and acknowledge our historical diversity, even forgiving the ways such history may have been dreadfully harmful.

What parts of your cultural history are you most likely to be ashamed of or ignore?

Of what parts of your cultural history are you most proud?

How can gospel humility lead to loving your neighbor as yourself, despite cultural differences?

Obviously, we're not attempting to deny the clear differences that exist between diverse people. Instead, what we must advocate is a gospel-rich confession that we compose one race. When that reality is clear, we're at a better starting point for discussing our differences.

When we come to understand this fact, we realize that most discussions in our culture about race and racism begin from a gospel-less starting point, for in the process of discussing our diversity in terms of different "races," we're undercutting our unity in the human race. And this isn't merely an issue of semantics. In our conversations we're creating categories for defining one another that are not only unhelpful but also eventually impossible.

The category of "race" as we commonly use it is unhelpful because it locates identity in physical appearance: "You're black; I'm white." These statements seem simple, but they're more than mere indicators of skin color. They carry with them a whole host of stereotypes and assumptions that are based squarely on biological attributes. Simply because skin tone or hair texture appear a certain way, we instinctively assume certain characteristics about others, either positively or negatively (most often negatively).

Read Ephesians 3:14-21.

What does Scripture reiterate about every family on earth?

What did Paul pray for every Christian?

For the church?

How does this prayer counter any attitudes of racism or prejudice?

IMMIGRATION

Read 1 Peter 2:11.

How are Christians identified in this verse?

We're all immigrants ourselves, aren't we? This isn't merely referring to the fact that our ancestors migrated to this country many years ago. This idea is the very essence of what it means to be a Christian. The Bible calls believers in Christ "sojourners and exiles" who "desire a better country" and "are seeking a homeland," a "city that is to come" (1 Pet. 2:11; Heb. 11:13-16; 13:14). In other words, Christians are migrants on this earth, and the more we get involved in the lives of immigrants, the better we'll understand the gospel.

How does this idea of being an alien in a world that isn't our home relate to what you studied yesterday about heaven?

God gave laws to His people, the ethnic Israelites, for their treatment of diverse people in their midst. After the Israelites spent centuries of exile in Egypt, God commanded them, "You shall not wrong a sojourner or oppress him, for you were sojourners in the land of Egypt" (Ex. 22:21). In language that follows on the heels of what we already examined in week 4 about justice for orphans and widows, God declared that He "loves the sojourner, giving him food and clothing," and He consequently called His people to "love the sojourner … for you were sojourners in the land of Egypt" (Deut. 10:18-19). Through the prophets God accused His people of extortion and robbery. "They have oppressed the poor and needy," God said, "and have extorted from the sojourner without justice" (Ezek. 22:29; also see Jer. 7:6; Zech. 7:10).

The Hebrew word for *sojourner* in these passages can be translated basically and understood practically as *immigrant*. These foreigners who'd been separated from their families and land found themselves in need of help from the people among whom they lived. As a result, God viewed them with particular compassion. Throughout Scripture the sojourner, or immigrant, is often grouped alongside the orphan and the widow. The pages of the Old Testament present God as "the LORD [who] watches over the sojourners" (Ps. 146:9).

In the New Testament Jesus—God with us—entered the scene as an illegal immigrant. Fleeing a brutal political situation in Bethlehem after He was born, Jesus' family traveled to Egypt, where they lived for years as sojourners in a foreign land. On Jesus' return to Israel and from the start of His ministry, He subtly subverted the national pride of ethnic Israelites who were anticipating a Jewish Messiah who would overthrow Rome and reestablish Israel. Though Jesus' primary focus was on "the lost sheep of the house of Israel" (Matt. 15:24), He nevertheless reached beyond national boundaries at critical moments to love, serve, teach, heal, and save Canaanites and Samaritans, Greeks and Romans. Then Jesus shocked the preconceived systems of His Jewish disciples, not only by dying on a cross and rising from the grave but also by commanding them to proclaim "repentance and forgiveness of sins ... in his name to all nations" (Luke 24:47). Jesus hadn't come just as the Savior and Lord of Israel; He had come as the Savior and Lord over all.

> **What's the undeniable conclusion about God's heart for people of all nations, including and especially the immigrant?**

If the God of the Bible possesses particular compassion for immigrants, even equating them with orphans and widows, and if the cross of Christ is designed to compel outreach across ethnic divisions, then how much more should we, as the people of God, care for immigrants from other countries in our midst?

FROM COVER TO COVER, SCRIPTURE TELLS THE STORY OF A GOD WHO LOVINGLY CARES FOR PEOPLE.

DAY 5
A GOSPEL RESPONSE TO ISSUES OF RACE

God's Word reminds us that, regardless of the color of our skin, we all have the same roots. Fundamentally, we're all part of the same human race. That's why we all need the same gospel.

Consider the starting point in the gospel for so many of the social issues we've addressed: the creation of man and woman in the image of God with equal dignity before God. As we've seen, this means that no human being is more or less human than another. Every person is made in God's image. Nothing short of disbelief in this gospel truth has led to the unthinkable horrors throughout history. Around the world, in different periods of time, these crimes against humanity were all born from demonic deception of leaders and citizens who believed that certain people are inherently superior to others who are intrinsically inferior—not just inferior but even less than human.

The danger of dehumanizing others for any reason is a slippery slope down which person after person and culture after culture for generation after generation has stumbled into grave destruction. Yet, from the very first chapter of the Bible, this much is clear: all men and all women are made in the very likeness of God.

How does this recurring foundational truth that all people are created in the image of God shape your view of humanity?

What variable negates the commonality of God's image in a person (skin color, physical ability, intelligence, personality, language, wealth, benefit, place of birth, religious belief, political conviction, temperament, etc.)?

How is race often misdefined from the beginning, undercutting commonalities to emphasize artificial differences?

What's helpful in understanding groups of people, not for the sake of stereotyping and isolating ourselves from them, but in order to organize and engage them in meaningful ways, particularly with the gospel? To use the language of Genesis 10, studied earlier this week, we compose "clans" in separate "nations" that speak different "languages" in diverse "lands."

Applied to our own setting in the United States, it makes no sense, then, to categorize our own country as a nation of black, white, brown, or other "races." Instead, we're a nation composed of increasingly diverse people groups. We are Anglo Americans, African Americans, Latin Americans, Asian Americans, and more. These categories can be subdivided further, based on other ethnolinguistic factors, leading us to the realization that we're a nation of unique people groups with diverse histories from different lands with distinct customs and even languages. Surely this rich diversity of people can't be adequately defined by skin tone, hair texture, or eye color alone.

Some might say that in abandoning categories of black and white in discussions of race and racism, we're trying to sweep under the rug centuries of history and oppression as if they never happened. By no means! Instead, by basing our dialogue more meaningfully on ethnolinguistic characteristics, we're acknowledging those real centuries of history and oppression, combined with a host of other fluid factors that can't be reduced to basic biology. Moreover, in removing race and racism from the discussion altogether, we're paving the way for us as one race to call racism what it actually is: sin born in a heart of pride and prejudice. And in doing this, we're setting the stage for understanding how the gospel is uniquely able to foster powerful unity in the middle of pervasive diversity.

The cultural division between Jews and Gentiles (non-Jews) was deep during the first century. Yet as the story of the church unfolds, we read that Gentiles began believing in Jesus, to many Jews' surprise. At first Jewish Christians didn't know how to respond. Should they accept even Gentile Christians? If so, did they need to impose Jewish customs on them? Though Gentiles were finally accepted into the church, they felt at best like second-class Christians.

Read Ephesians 2:12-14.

According to these verses, remembering what theological truth should affect our attitudes toward and treatment of people from different backgrounds? Summarize this truth in your own words.

Read Ephesians 2:18-19.

These words beautifully describe the unique power of the gospel to reunite people from (and, for that matter, within) different ethnic groups. And it makes sense, doesn't it? For in the beginning sin separated man and woman from God and also from each other. This sin is at the root of ethnic pride and prejudice. When Christ went to the cross, He conquered sin, making the way for men and women to be free from it and restored to God. In so doing, He paved the way for men and women to be reconciled to one another. Followers of Christ thus have one "Father" as one family in one "household," with no "dividing wall of hostility" based on ethnic diversity.

Where do you see the greatest division in our culture today? In your church?

Amid necessary political discussions and inevitable personal disagreements, first and foremost the gospel reminds us that when we're talking about immigrants (legal or illegal), we're talking about men and women made in the image of God and pursued by the grace of God. Consequently, followers of Christ with faith in God must see immigrants not as problems to be solved but as people to be loved. The gospel compels us to decry any and all forms of oppression, exploitation, bigotry, or harassment of immigrants, regardless of their legal status. These are men and women for whom Christ died, and their dignity is no greater or less than our own. Likewise, their families are no less important than our own.

As part of the Father's household, we're called to love our neighbors. And even though we live for the sake of an eternal home, we're still citizens within communities today. So how do we live for God's glory "on earth as it is in heaven" (Matt. 6:10)?

Fiery debate has raged across the United States about how to address the 12 to 15 million undocumented immigrants currently living in our country. These men, women, and children live in our communities, representing various ethnicities, speaking different languages, and coming from different cultural backgrounds.

By the grace of God, we must work to overcome prejudicial pride in our lives, families, and churches, a process that begins with changing the conversation about race altogether. Moreover, with the wisdom of God, we must labor to respect immigration laws in our country as responsible citizens while loving immigrant souls in our community as compassionate Christians.

Read Romans 13:1-10.

Where do you struggle with submitting to political authority? Why?

If you're tempted to dismiss the convicting truths of these verses, consider the fact this was written to Roman Christians during the reign of Nero.

How can your attitude toward the government be a countercultural testimony of your humility before God, regardless of what politician holds an office?

The Bible clearly teaches that government exists under God to establish and enforce laws for the good of people. We have a responsibility before God as citizens under a government to work together to establish and enforce just laws that address immigration.

How can respectfully working within political channels be a means by which you love your neighbor as yourself, regardless of ethnicity or citizenship?

There aren't easy answers to the complex issues of immigration, but the gospel requires Christians to wrestle with these questions. Regardless of personal or political views, none of us can escape the reality that we're talking about our neighbors, and Jesus' command regarding our neighbors is clear. As long as immigrants, legal and illegal, live around us by God's sovereign design (see Acts 17:26-27), we're compelled to consider how to love them as we love ourselves (see Luke 10:25-37).

How does the gospel shape what you believe about race? Record a simple statement of what you believe.

How does the gospel shape what you believe about immigration? Record a simple statement of what you believe.

How do conversations about race or immigration open doors to share the gospel? Record a simple statement explaining how this particular issue is rooted in a foundational understanding of the gospel and our relationship with God.

Identify a specific time when you've been in a conversation or incident related to issues of race or the topic of immigration. Describe the conversation and your perceived outcome.

Following this study, would you say or do anything differently?   YES   NO
How will you approach this issue in the future?

WEEK 6
FAITH

WELCOME TO THIS FINAL GROUP DISCUSSION OF *COUNTER CULTURE*.

What was most helpful, encouraging, or challenging in your study of week 5?

What issues of faith, religious belief, or persecution have you seen in the news lately? Share a recent news story related to faith or religious persecution.

To prepare to view the DVD segment, read aloud 2 Corinthians 4:13-18.

Since we have the same spirit of faith according to what has been written, "I believed, and so I spoke," we also believe, and so we also speak, knowing that he who raised the Lord Jesus will raise us also with Jesus and bring us with you into his presence. For it is all for your sake, so that as grace extends to more and more people it may increase thanksgiving, to the glory of God. So we do not lose heart. Though our outer self is wasting away, our inner self is being renewed day by day. For this light momentary affliction is preparing for us an eternal weight of glory beyond all comparison, as we look not to the things that are seen but to the things that are unseen. For the things that are seen are transient, but the things that are unseen are eternal.
2 Corinthians 4:13-18

COMPLETE THE VIEWER GUIDE BELOW AS YOU WATCH DVD SESSION 6.

1. As we believe the gospel with deep-seated _____ in our lives, let's proclaim the gospel with death-defying _____ in the world.

   • Those who _____ the gospel _____ the gospel.

   • We're compelled to proclaim the resurrected Christ to unreached peoples, knowing that as we speak the gospel to them, _____ and affliction will come.

   • _____ follows proclamation.

   • We go because God _____ to us.

2. As we live to _____ God's grace among more people, let's long to _____ God's glory among all peoples.

   • We extend the grace of God so that people are delivered from everlasting condemnation away from God to experience everlasting _____ in the presence of God.

   • As people are saved, God will receive more _____, more thanksgiving.

   • What drives passion for getting the gospel to unreached peoples is not guilt; it's _____.

3. As we continually envision eternal _____ with God, let's joyfully embrace earthly _____ from God.

   • There's a god in this world who wants to _____ every single one of our minds and the minds of the nations from seeing God.

   • There's a true God over this world who desires the _____ of all peoples in the world.

   • Suffering is inevitable.

     The more passionate we are about spreading the gospel in the world, the more we will _____.

     God will pass us by as long as we value _____ over obedience.

   • God's purpose is _____.

   • Our hope is _____.

Video sessions available for purchase at *www.lifeway.com/counterculture*

DISCUSS THE DVD SEGMENT WITH YOUR GROUP, USING THE QUESTIONS BELOW.

What was most helpful, encouraging, or challenging in this session? Why?

Why is it fair to refer to people who don't have access to the gospel as the greatest social injustice of our day?

What clear call has God given to all His people?

When, where, or around whom are you tempted to believe that faith should be private—that you don't need to talk about the gospel?

In what ways are you tempted to lose heart in living out and sharing your faith in our culture? Among the nations? How will you fight losing heart?

What's the difference between being motivated by guilt and by glory?

How does your view of people change when you believe there's a cosmic spiritual battle with a little-g god blinding people to the light of the gospel?

David said ultimately everything comes down to the question "Do you really believe this gospel?" How does this question change your life? How does it relate to the way you understand and respond to social issues?

How do issues of religious freedom and persecution open a door to conversations about the gospel? Give examples of statements that can be used to share the gospel in conversations about religious freedom and persecution.

Overall, what's been the most significant thing you've learned during this study?

THIS WEEK

Identify at least one person with whom you'll share the gospel this week. Ask God to provide opportunities to share what you've studied these past six weeks. Pray for boldness and humility in discussing and applying the gospel when you encounter these various controversial issues. Memorize 2 Corinthians 4:13-14.

READ week 6 and complete the activities to conclude your study of *Counter Culture.*
READ chapters 9–10 in the book *Counter Culture* by David Platt (Tyndale, 2015).

FAITH

Since we have the same spirit of faith according to what has been written, "I believed, and so I spoke," we also believe, and so we also speak, knowing that he who raised the Lord Jesus will raise us also with Jesus and bring us with you into his presence.
2 Corinthians 4:13-14

"Believing that further delay would be sinful, some of God's insignificants and nobodies in particular, but trusting in our Omnipotent God, have decided on certain simple lines, according to the Book of God, to make a definite attempt to render the evangelization of the world an accomplished fact. ... Too long have we been waiting for one another to begin! The time for waiting is past! The hour of God has struck! ... In God's Holy Name let us arise and build! ... We will not build on the sand, but on the bedrock of the sayings of Christ, and the gates and minions of hell shall not prevail against us. Should such men as we fear? Before the whole world, aye, before the sleepy, lukewarm, faithless, namby-pamby Christian world, we will dare to trust our God, with His joy unspeakable singing aloud in our hearts. We will a thousand times sooner die trusting only in our God, than live trusting in man. And when we come to this position the battle is already won, and the end of the glorious campaign in sight. We will have the real Holiness of God, not the sickly stuff of talk and dainty words and pretty thoughts; we will have a [real] Holiness, one of daring faith and works for Jesus Christ."
C.T. Studd

In this final week we'll focus on the greatest social injustice in the world today and see that every cultural issue—no matter how controversial—is ultimately a matter of believing and applying the gospel to our lives.

1. C.T. Studd, "Christ's Nobodies," as quoted in *The Intercessor*, vol. 26, no. 4 [online, cited 1 December 2014].
    Available from the Internet: *zerubbabel.org*.

FREEDOM

As you enter this final week of study, you must settle this final question: How will you respond to those who don't believe what you believe?

It's inevitable that people disagree with one another. Yet a Christian's desire for other people should be twofold.

1. We desire that others join us in faith, sharing our belief in the gospel of Jesus.

2. We respect those who don't share our belief.

For both of these desires we must be unapologetic and unwavering. If we believe the gospel is true, then of course we desire for others to likewise experience the joy of salvation and the hope of eternal life in relationship with our Creator and Father through faith in Jesus, His only Son.

Likewise, based on everything we've studied—all people being created in the image of God, with equal dignity and worth, regardless of gender, ethnicity, or other factors—we respect every man and woman. Without condoning sin or affirming values, beliefs, and behaviors contrary to God's Word, we love our neighbors as ourselves.

Read Luke 6:31-33.

How does Jesus' command apply not only to personal relationships but also to religious liberty in our culture?

Today let's focus primarily on this second part of our interaction with a culture and individuals who possess different values and beliefs. This is the more difficult of the two stated desires as Christians. Later we'll focus on the obvious overflow of our hearts to share what we're most passionate about.

Yet again, this week's issue leads us back to the beginning of the Bible, where God created man in His image with a unique ability to know Him. Consequently, one of the fundamental human freedoms—if not the most fundamental human freedom—is each person's opportunity to explore truth about God and to live in light of his or her determinations. It's an essential part of the human experience to ask and answer questions like "Where did I come from? Why am I here? How should I live my life?" And it's each person's God-given right to live according to his or her conclusions. Obviously, different people will make different determinations about what to believe, whom to worship, and how to live. But God allows that freedom.

Early in Old Testament history God miraculously led His people out of slavery from Egypt. He literally set them free and was leading them to a new life as a nation of people called out and set apart for His glory in all the earth. Yet the human heart is fickle and ungrateful. We're naturally selfish creatures. Even today, much like the Israelites back then, people desire comfort and ease over the purposes of God. And even today God still gives us a choice.

Read Joshua 24:14-15.

What choice were God's people commanded to make?

How do people—maybe even you at times—try to live in our culture without making a firm decision as to what to believe about God?

This reality becomes even clearer in the rest of Scripture, specifically in the life and ministry of Jesus. Never do we see Jesus forcing faith onto people. Instead, He taught doctrine, told stories, and then invited men and women to receive or reject Him. In response, people listened to Him, reasoned with Him, argued with Him, disagreed with Him, abandoned Him, and then eventually killed Him.

Read Luke 9:51-56.

When have you wanted someone who rejected you or your beliefs to face judgment?

Jesus rebuked His disciples for their worldly attitude, which was likely fueled by both religious and ethnic differences with the Samaritans. Then, when He sent the disciples out on mission, He encouraged them to respect people's freedom to reject them (see Luke 10:5-11). We see, then, that regardless of one's perspective on the doctrines of election and free will, there's no question that the language of the Bible indicates the importance of willful choice and personal invitation. In the end the gospel message is fundamentally a matter of invitation, not coercion. "Behold, I stand at the door and knock," Jesus says at the close of Scripture. "If anyone hears my voice and opens the door, I will come in to him and eat with him, and he with me" (Rev. 3:20).

Nobody is forced to believe. True faith can't be forced.

We must remember that we're not exclusively talking about freedom for Christians in our culture. The same right to religious liberty that should protect followers of Christ should also protect followers of any other religion or of none at all.

In what ways have you seen culture demonize intolerance?

In what areas are Christians deemed intolerant?

What's the irony of culture denying Christian expression deemed as intolerant?

Our culture's view of tolerance is problematic. Tolerance is the ultimate virtue in our culture. One could even argue that tolerance has been not only idealized but also idolized. Everyone is expected to bow down to this supreme good. Therefore, the ultimate cultural "sin" is to disagree with another person's core values. Believing you're right and another person is wrong about something as personal as faith or the other issues we've studied is labeled hateful and intolerant. The culture simply won't tolerate intolerance. While we make light of this thinking in order to make a point, it's anything but a joke.

Christians who dare to counter culture are increasingly being viewed as hateful, offensive, narrow-minded, bigoted, and intolerant.

Yet by definition tolerance can exist only when there's disagreement. We have to disagree with someone in order to tolerate them. We also have to realize that tolerating people and tolerating beliefs are two different things. Tolerating people requires that we treat one another with equal value, dignity, and respect, recognizing that everybody has a right to their beliefs.

On the other hand, tolerating beliefs doesn't require the acceptance of every idea as equally valid. We don't have to believe that anything is equally true, right, or good simply because it's expressed by someone of equal dignity. Being tolerant of a person's value doesn't mean you must accept that person's views.

For example, you can have a Muslim friend whom you respect deeply yet disagree with passionately. As a Christian, you believe Jesus is the Son of God; a Muslim doesn't. Muslims believe Muhammad was a prophet sent from God; Christians don't believe this. Christians believe Jesus died on a cross and rose from the grave for the forgiveness of our sins; Muslims don't share this belief. They believe they'll go to heaven when they die without faith in Jesus as their Savior; Christians believe Jesus said He's the only way to heaven.

These are major points of disagreement, and they shouldn't be minimized. The tendency in our culture is to say, "Whatever you believe is right for you." But such thinking simply can't apply to any of the previous issues. Either Jesus is or isn't the Son of God. He can't be the Son of God and not be the Son of God at the same time. Similarly, either Muhammad was a prophet sent from God, or he wasn't. Either Jesus died on the cross and rose from the grave, or He didn't. Muslims will either go to heaven when they die, or they won't.

These are serious questions of eternal significance, and the purpose of religious freedom is to provide an atmosphere in which these questions can be explored. Thank God for the opportunity you currently have to express and exercise your faith. Don't take this freedom for granted. Likewise, don't settle for this right to apply only to yourself and those who believe as you do.

How does what you've studied about human life, dignity, and the image of God affect your view of tolerance toward individuals?

Record a prayer asking for humility as you interact with people for the sake of the gospel.

DAY 2
OUR MISSION

From cover to cover, the purpose of God's people, as presented in Scripture, has always been to fill the earth with His glory.

This was true in the beginning; it will be true in the end. Jesus reiterated our mission following His death, burial, and resurrection.

Read Matthew 28:1-10.

To whom did Jesus first appear after His resurrection from the dead?

What had the angel told them, and what did Jesus tell them?

Not only had Jesus overcome sin and death in His resurrection, but He also countered culture in the very way He made the good news known. It's no coincidence that women were the first to witness the resurrected Lord. This isn't a minor detail. It's revolutionary. Culturally, women weren't seen as possessing equal worth as men. Time and time again, God proved His love for all people in profound ways. These two Jewish women—Mary Magdalene and Mary—were the first people Jesus sent out to spread the good news of His resurrection. The gospel is the great equalizer.

Read Matthew 28:16-17.

What doubts do you still wrestle with in your faith? How can you lay those at the feet of Jesus in worship?

Notice that the women were commanded by the angel and by Jesus to instruct the disciples to meet Jesus in Galilee. Obedience accompanied their experience. It was after the women and disciples responded to the command to go that they experienced Jesus in His glory. Jesus went to them in their obedience, even in their fear and doubt.

Read Matthew 28:18-20.

Why is it significant that before giving the disciples the Great Commission, Jesus began with the statement in verse 18?

What exactly did Jesus command?

What promise did Jesus provide at the end of verse 20?

The imperative in that sentence is "make disciples." That's our command. Every disciple is called to make more disciples. We're to do this as we go—wherever we are and anywhere the Spirit leads. This isn't a professional job description in the sense that only salaried employees of churches and mission organizations are to make disciples. If every disciple is taught to obey everything Jesus commands, that includes this command to "go therefore and make disciples" (v. 19). We do this because Jesus has "all authority in heaven and on earth" (v. 18). We do this in the confidence of that same reality and His promise to be with us as we go.

Yesterday we looked at how to respond to a culture and to individuals who don't share our belief in the gospel. Here we see that our greatest desire and God's expectation are to share the gospel, extending God's grace to others and exalting God's glory in our culture.

Read 2 Corinthians 4:1-7.

In what way are you overwhelmed or tempted to lose heart when you think about making disciples in your own culture and in every nation?

Where have you seen cunning or tampering with God's Word (see v. 2) to make being a Christian seem more appealing to our culture?

How are treasure and light (see vv. 4–7) appropriate metaphors for the gospel?

Is that the desire of your heart? Do you truly want the church in our day to join together and make a definite attempt under the sovereign grace of our God to render the evangelization of the world an accomplished fact? It's possible. Not only is it possible, but it's also promised. It will happen. Every nation will be reached with the gospel successfully, for we know that around the throne in heaven, every tribe, tongue, and nation will give glory to God (see Rev. 7:9-10).

This isn't to say we can pull ourselves up by our bootstraps to complete the Great Commission in our own power and strength. We aren't sovereign over the results of our efforts to make disciples in every nation, but our sovereign God has given us a specific goal, and it's clear. He's commanded His people to make the gospel known among all nations—all the ethnic groups of the world. And He's given us a promise—His very presence, the power of His Spirit in us—to accomplish that purpose.

Right now as you read this, there are 6,500 people groups in the world, representing two billion people who aren't experiencing the grace of God or giving glory to God.

So let's not stay silent with this gospel.

We don't have to ask what the will of God is in the world. He wants His people to provide for the poor, to value the unborn, to care for orphans and widows, to defend marriage, to war against sexual immorality in all its forms in every area of our lives, to rescue people from slavery, to proclaim and practice truth regardless of the risk, to love our neighbors as ourselves regardless of their ethnicity, and to proclaim the gospel to all nations. Of these things we're sure. Ultimately, God desires disciples to be made of every nation. Jesus commanded it. And He promised to go with us to accomplish it.

Go and do these things, not because you have a sense of guilt that you ought to act but because you have a passion for the gospel that makes you want to act. Do them because you know you were once impoverished in your sin, a slave to Satan, orphaned, and alone in this world. Yet God reached down with His grace-filled hand into your sin-soaked heart, and through the sacrifice of His only begotten Son on a blood-stained cross, He lifted you up to new life by His alluring love. You now have nothing to fear and nothing to lose because you're robed in the riches of Christ and safe in the security of Christ.

There's nothing you as an individual or everyone working together can do to rid this world of pain and suffering. That responsibility belongs to the resurrected Christ, and He will do it when He returns. But until that day, do with an undivided heart whatever He calls you to do.

Believe with all your heart that God has put you in this culture at this time for a reason. He's called you to Himself, saved you by His Son, and filled you with His Spirit. He's captured you with His love, and He's compelling you by His Word to go into the world proclaiming the kingdom of God. And don't be worried about what it will cost you in the culture around you, because you're confident deep down inside that, in the gospel, God Himself is your great reward.

How does our mission as the church relate to what was studied last week about ethnic diversity and unity?

What are you personally doing to make disciples of all nations?

How is your small group joining your church to fulfill the Great Commission?

DAY 3
PERSONAL BUT NOT PRIVATE

God's Word is clear. Personal experience echoes the same fact. Our lives are on display.

We have become a spectacle to the world, to angels, and to men.
1 Corinthians 4:9

The world is watching. Children. Parents. Neighbors. Coworkers. Teammates. Classmates. Friends. Acquaintances. Not to mention the fact that our culture encourages the sharing of virtually every other part of our lives through social media. It seems that most in our culture are eager to make public every detail of their personal lives and to share opinions, preferences, and beliefs on almost anything other than the gospel. Because it's inherently controversial.

The gospel must challenge people. It must convict. People must face the reality of their sin and judgment in order to fall on the grace of God, submit to the will of our Lord, and humbly receive the sacrifice of the Lamb. But while the reality of sinfulness is convicting and uncomfortable, to say the least, the good news of Jesus' work to redeem us is liberating and motivating.

People are watching to see how you live. You're a spectacle. A marvel. A wonder of the world. The Christian life will counter culture. By definition and design the people of God are called to be in the world but not of it (see John 17:11,16). Jesus prayed that God would unify the church in the generations following His time on earth so that the watching world would see their lives and the love they shared and believe the gospel.

Therefore, we don't merely aim to lead polite, moral lives in the hopes that someone may be attracted to saving faith in Jesus because we're nice. As Christians, we live for more than ourselves. We must. We live for a kingdom and a home that aren't of this world. We live for a Father, Creator, Redeemer, and King who loves us and satisfies us in a way that's far greater—and far more real—than anything in this temporal world.

When have you said or been told that faith is a private matter?

What reasons are given in our culture to justify keeping quiet about personal faith and religious belief?

How would you explain that faith must be personal but not private?

Read 1 Corinthians 1:18-25.

What does Scripture reveal about cultural preferences and human thought?

What about the gospel seems foolish or hard to believe in our culture?

Read 1 Corinthians 1:26-31.

What encouragement does this Scripture give you in the face of judgment, criticism, and ridicule for believing the gospel?

How can (and should) a Christian be personally humble yet boast in the Lord?

Our culture wants to insist that it's unloving and unwise to even speak of our belief that Jesus is the only way to be saved. Many have been deceived into believing that any conversation or action that could influence or encourage another person's faith is manipulative. People are being taught that ultimate truth comes from within through no external pressure. While this may sound noble in ways, any reasonable person would have to admit that it's impossible to live and think without so-called outside influences. We've already seen that our culture increasingly believes that individuals should make up their own minds about gender, sexuality, and marriage. It should be no surprise that those who follow the wisdom of this world also desire to make up their own minds about what sort of God would fit their preferences.

Our nation's Declaration of Independence starts with these words:

> "We hold these truths to be self-evident, that all men are created equal, that they are endowed by their Creator with certain unalienable Rights, that among these are Life, Liberty and the pursuit of Happiness."

The founders of our country called faith a fundamental human right—indeed, the very first human right. In order to ensure the protection of these rights, our nation's founders went on to draft the Bill of Rights, the first of which reads:

> "Congress shall make no law respecting an establishment of religion, or prohibiting the free exercise thereof."

In putting this right first, our founders acknowledged that freedom of religion is the foundation for all other freedoms. After all, if government can mandate what you believe or deny you the opportunity to live within your beliefs, then where will its reach end? What would keep it from dictating what you can read or write, what you can hear or say, or how you must live? The founders concluded that if God Himself doesn't violate the religious freedom of man, government shouldn't either.

As we saw in day 1 of this week, it's our God-given right to choose what we believe and how we live. We've seen that from the beginning of human history, God hasn't forced Himself on people. Man and woman were given freedom. However, we also see that their freedom didn't remove their responsibility. In fact, because they had freedom, they were responsible for their decisions about the truth and authority of God over their lives. Their freedom also didn't remove any outside authority. Quite the opposite. The very first sin occurred when man and woman determined what was good for themselves. Believing that right and wrong can be determined apart from the authority of God outside ourselves is not only foolish but also damning. This isn't a new cultural phenomenon. This is the recurring theme of history and the natural pattern of every human heart.

Where our culture twists this freedom—this unalienable right—and takes it too far is at the understanding of personal faith. Commonly known as the "freedom to worship," this label can be somewhat misleading because the way it's often applied in our culture unnecessarily and unhelpfully limits the "free exercise" of religion to our private lives.

When people hear "freedom to worship," they often envision the freedom for men, women, and children to gather together in a church building, synagogue, mosque, or another place for corporate worship. This picture may also extend to the home, where families have the freedom to pray (or not to pray) at mealtimes, before bed, or at other times during the day. But even so, all this is private, a religious freedom limited to what happens when someone is alone or in a specific gathering of a physical family or a faith family.

What this label fails to acknowledge is that those who gather for worship in private settings then scatter to live out their beliefs in the public square. As men, women, and children live, study, work, and play in every sector of society, they perform duties and make decisions in alignment with their consciences and in accordance with their convictions. This is a part of the "free exercise" of religion: the freedom to worship not just in episodic gatherings but in everyday life. And it's such "free exercise" that's subtly yet significantly being attacked in American culture today.

Freedom of religion becomes freedom from religion. The mantra of our culture has become that each person has the right to believe what they want to believe and also has the right not to be exposed to what anyone else believes. People are free to worship privately as long as they keep it to themselves. Consequently, the public sphere—culture—should be void of religion. Spiritual matters of faith and truth are personal—meaning private—according to our culture. Anybody who dares live out their faith or talk about their beliefs, especially in any way that would invite others to adopt their faith, are seen not as those freely exercising their own religion but as violating another person's right. Do you see what's happening?

Yet this is nothing new. And as Christians, we can't be silent.

Read 2 Corinthians 4:13-15.

What will we do if we truly believe the gospel—the power of the resurrected Lord?

What's our twofold purpose regarding grace and glory? Who's the recipient of each?

WE BELIEVE. SO WE SPEAK.

DAY 4
PERSECUTION

We can be sure that the gospel will reach the ends of the earth and disciples will be made of all nations. It's inevitable in God's perfect timing. It's also inevitable, in a world bent toward idolatry and rebellion against God, that we'll face hardship as we go. So how does the gospel compel us to live in a world where many of our brothers and sisters are suffering for their faith in Christ?

Followers of Christ compose the most widely persecuted religious group in the world. According to the U.S. Department of State, Christians face persecution of some kind in more than 60 different countries today. On the whole, about three hundred Christians around the world are killed every month for their faith in Christ[1] (and some estimates give a higher number). Literally countless others are persecuted through abuse; beatings; imprisonment; torture; and deprivation of food, water, and shelter. Each occurrence of religious oppression represents an individual story of faith tested amid fire and trial. But these aren't merely stories on a page. They are brothers and sisters in Christ. They are children of our Heavenly Father, created in the image of God, redeemed by the blood of Jesus.

Think about why persecution like this happens. It's not because Christians in other countries have a secret faith they keep to themselves. As long as a Christian is quiet about his or her faith in Christ—not saying anything to anyone about Christ but praying and practicing faith in privacy—then that Christian faces far less risk of persecution. It's only when a Christian is public about his or her faith—applying faith in the public square and even proclaiming Christ—that persecution will inevitably occur.

Read 2 Corinthians 11:24-27.

How does Paul's description of his experience fly in the face of our culture—even church culture—that believing or doing the right things will result in a comfortable life?

Paul wrote about all he'd endured in prison—beaten, near death, five times receiving 40 lashes minus 1, three times beaten with rods, stoned once. In danger from Jews, in danger from Gentiles, in danger in the city, in danger in the wilderness, often without food, in cold and exposure. All this was a direct result of proclaiming Christ throughout Asia.

Read 2 Corinthians 1:3-9.

What's Paul's comfort in the midst of suffering?

In Paul's experience what two positive things come from suffering?

When have you been comforted or been able to comfort someone in a way that revealed the loving presence of God?

All the suffering here was tied to Paul's proclamation of the gospel in Asia. And the suffering threatened to hinder his proclamation of the gospel to different nations.

The context of this passage is mission among difficult peoples in dangerous places. Paul believed, so he spoke, knowing suffering, affliction, and persecution would come, yet knowing God, who raised the Lord Jesus, would also raise us with Him.

On a less severe but very real way, we're beginning to face persecution and have our freedom to exercise our religion threatened in our culture. Most noticeably, Christian convictions based on God's design for life—including marriage, gender, sexuality, and the value of unborn children—are bringing business owners into conflict with culture. This conflict results in social, financial, and even legal consequences.

Scores of men and women from many faiths, including many of our brothers and sisters in Christ, live today without the kind of liberty we're considering. And for cultures around the world, millions upon millions of people are presently denied the opportunity to even explore truth that will affect their lives on earth and for eternity.

A principle can be identified from simply observing our world and God's Word: persecution follows proclamation. Suffering for the gospel accompanies spreading the gospel:

> *We are fools for Christ's sake, but you are wise in Christ. We are weak, but you are strong. You are held in honor, but we in disrepute. To the present hour we hunger and thirst, we are poorly dressed and buffeted and homeless, and we labor, working with our own hands. When reviled, we bless; when persecuted, we endure; when slandered, we entreat. We have become, and are still, like the scum of the world, the refuse of all things.*
> 1 Corinthians 4:10-13

When have you suffered isolation, ridicule, or persecution for your faith in Jesus or biblical convictions as a Christian?

None of this surprises our Lord, however. "Blessed are those who are persecuted for righteousness' sake, for theirs is the kingdom of heaven," Jesus told His disciples. "Blessed are you when others revile you and persecute you and utter all kinds of evil against you falsely on my account. Rejoice and be glad, for your reward is great in heaven" (Matt. 5:10-12). On a later occasion, when He sent these disciples out like "sheep in the midst of wolves," He promised them that persecution would come: "Beware of men, for they will deliver you over to courts and flog you in their synagogues, and you will be dragged before governors and kings for my sake, to bear witness before them." He concluded, "You will be hated … for my name's sake. But the one who endures to the end will be saved" (Matt. 10:16-18,22). Even a quick reading of Gospel passages like these reveals that the more we become like Jesus in this world, the more we'll experience what He experienced.

Read 2 Corinthians 4:16-18.

How is your inner self being renewed each day?

What perspective does this Scripture provide on our lives and suffering?

Suffering can't silence the spirit of faith. Even in the midst of affliction and suffering, we believe, and so we speak. We have a greater reward than any fleeting pleasure or relief in this world. Jesus is worthy of our lives. He's our greatest joy. We gladly endure any circumstance for the sake of His grace and glory:

> *That which was from the beginning, which we have heard, which we have seen with our eyes, which we looked upon and have touched with our hands, concerning the word of life—the life was made manifest, and we have seen it, and testify to it and proclaim to you the eternal life, which was with the Father and was made manifest to us—that which we have seen and heard we proclaim also to you, so that you too may have fellowship with us; and indeed our fellowship is with the Father and with his Son Jesus Christ. And we are writing these things so that our joy may be complete.*
> 1 John 1:1-4

WE BELIEVE THE GOSPEL WITH DEEP-SEATED CONVICTION IN OUR LIVES. LET'S PROCLAIM THE GOSPEL WITH DEATH-DEFYING CONFIDENCE IN THE WORLD.

1. "About Christian Persecution," *Open Doors* [online, cited 3 December 2014]. Available from the Internet: *www.opendoorsusa.org/persecution/about-persecution*.

DAY 5
A GOSPEL RESPONSE TO ISSUES OF FAITH & PERSECUTION

The aim of this study isn't to make you an alarmist. But maybe it should be. Maybe an alarm needs to be sounded, and maybe all of us need to seriously consider how to apply gospel conviction in a rapidly shifting religious culture.

We're swimming in a culture that's increasingly hostile toward the gospel. We're surrounded by billions of people, thousands of people groups, who've never even heard the gospel. And while our own culture is increasingly hostile, other cultures around the world are violent. Though our own suffering is real, Christians around the world are facing persecution and even death.

The result of this global reality, along with a true gospel reverence, should be action. We must act. We must pray and work for our persecuted brothers and sisters around the world. In a land of religious liberty, we have a biblical responsibility to stand up and speak out on their behalf.

Read 1 Corinthians 12:26.

How does the analogy of a body help you understand persecution and empathize with the persecuted in this culture or with other believers throughout the world?

In a country where even our own religious liberty is increasingly limited, our suffering brothers and sisters beckon us not to let the cost of following Christ in our culture silence our faith. Privatized Christianity is no Christianity at all, for it's practically impossible to know Christ and not proclaim Christ: to believe His Word when we read it in our homes or churches and not obey it in our communities and cities. We must always remember that while our citizenship officially belongs to the government, our souls ultimately belong to God.

The oppression of the poor, the abortion of children, the neglect of orphans and widows, the trafficking of slaves, the significance of marriage and sexuality, the need for ethnic equality, and the importance of religious liberty are all mammoth issues in our lives, families, churches, and culture. The hope is that if you didn't feel a burden for these things before you started this study, you do now.

Please don't allow these burdens on your heart to terminate with this study after you close this book. Let the Spirit move. Allow these realities to transform the way you live. Don't waste the life God has granted you or the opportunities He's given you to apply the gospel by which He's saved you in the culture where He's placed you.

Read Luke 9:57-62.

These three men were potential followers of Jesus, but from all we can tell in this text, it seems as though Jesus talked them out of following Him. (This in and of itself is countercultural!) But this is essentially the decision you're faced with at this moment in the midst of your culture. Will you follow Jesus? Do you really believe He's worth it? Do you really believe the gospel? The question isn't, Are you going to bow your head, say a prayer, read the Bible, go to church, and give a tithe while you get on with the rest of your life? It all comes down to whether you're going to follow Jesus with all your life, no matter where He leads you to go; how much He calls you to give; or what the cost may be for you, your family, and your church.

Are you going to choose comfort or the cross? Are you going to settle for maintenance or sacrifice for mission? Will your life be marked by an indecisive mind or an undivided heart?

How does the gospel shape what you believe about personal faith and religious freedom? Record a simple statement of what you believe.

How does the gospel shape what you believe about religious persecution? Record a simple statement of what you believe.

How do conversations about religious liberty and persecution open doors to share the gospel? Record a simple statement explaining how this particular issue is rooted in a foundational understanding of the gospel and our relationship with God.

Identify a specific time when you've been in a conversation related to faith, religious liberty, or persecution. Describe the conversation and your perceived outcome.

Following this study, would you say or do anything differently?   YES   NO
How will you approach this issue in the future?

What's God calling you to do in response to His Word? What practical steps will you take to extend His grace to others and exalt His glory among your culture?

DEVOTED TO
CHRIST.
SERVING THE
CHURCH.
REACHING THE
NATIONS.

Radical.net

a resource ministry of
pastor and author
David Platt